GOD

IS

GOOD

Written by
Dr. Daney Dumdeang

Introduction

This treasured biblical book is a labor of love that I have worked on for decades, grounded in my sincere faith that Jesus is the Son of God. My spiritual journey began at a young age when I met Dr. Chawankorn, a missionary from Australia. He invited me to church, where I studied the Bible with him daily and worshipped every Sunday.

During those early days, I witnessed miraculous things occurring in the church almost every week. I saw the blind receive their sight and many other supernatural phenomena. Later, miracles began to occur in my own life as well. This book is based on those personal adventures, specifically the mission journey I took to India with my wife and daughter.

In these pages, you will find chapters on Christian worship and a collection of my writings and corrections compiled over many decades. I have also included biblical verses that have inspired me, along with personal Christmas testimonies that I was unable to include in my previous book. I am grateful for the opportunity to finally insert them here, emphasizing that this book is a work of spiritual sharing based on real, personal experiences.

My prayer is that you will receive a miracle that goes above and beyond the limitations of your own faith. To the Christian reader who has faith in Jesus—the Son of God who came to take away our sins and died on the cross—I hope this book inspires you to live a holy life, blessed by the Word of God.

I have prayed hard that these pages would reflect God's way, not my own. May this book become a treasure to you, providing daily peace of mind like medicine from God.

I am a Christian who believes that Jesus Christ is the Son of God, that God raised Him from the dead, and that those who live in unity with Christ will share in the same reward: eternal life. My task in writing this is based on my purified faith in Him. I trust that you, the reader, possess this same faith, which works within you even without your knowing—what I call the "Dynamics of Faith".

We must have absolute faith. This is the acceptance of being accepted. Of course, in a state of despair, it feels as though nobody and nothing accepts us; yet, there is the power of acceptance itself. It is my hope that this book will inspire and transform your life just as these truths have transformed mine. This is the mystery and the power of faith that I am sharing with you.

May God bless you all.

Faithfully,

Dr. Daney Dumdeang

Dedication

The author would like to profoundly dedicate this book to their lovely, sweet wife, who possesses a strong and stable faith in Jesus. Most of her friends have always honored her as "Saint Patty."

She has directly influenced me in my absolute Christian faith. She is not only my soulmate but my spiritual companion as well. I thank God for guiding me to be part of her life eternally.

With Love,

Dr. Daney Dumdeang

Dumdeang Foundation

Thankful Note

This book would not be complete without a few people in my life who gave me assistance and inspired me.

I thank Bob, my dear friend, who encouraged and inspired me while I was in the mission field in Sri Lanka and elsewhere. One of his emails said, "I am so happy and glad that even while you are on a mission, you are searching for God, studying the Word of God, and helping to heal others. I am proud to be your friend, my dear friend Dr. Daney." He has inspired me to devote my time and my life to serve God's work and His duty. What I have done until today, I have done not for myself, but for others and for the world of humanity.

I thank my three children and my eight wonderful grandchildren who always support me. Of course, I thank my lovely wife, who is always by my side giving me the greatest support.

I thank Luk Dej for the manuscripts the great Luk Dej.

Last but not least, I thank Sophie Brown, my great literary partner, for her support in kindly bringing this book to the book industry for a worldwide audience, along with all her team from Franklin Publishers.

Finally, I thank the readers who support me. I hope you see that this book is special and significant, and that it may guide the purpose of your life in following the words of God daily. God is good.

Warm Regards,

Dr. Daney Dumdeang

President of the Dumdeang Foundation

Table Of Content

Chapter 1

CHRISTIAN WORSHIP

November 22, 2004: Worship

At this point in the service, a voice cries out, "Let us pray." The worshippers now turn their attention to the future tasks of responsibility in and for the world.

December 1, 2004 at 7:46 AM

My daughter was tired and took time off to sleep in our resort hotel. My wife and I took a taxi to the Movement Teachers Conference, where we were invited as distinguished guests. There were over a thousand people in the audience, including over a hundred movement authorities and government officials.

The conference was held for training and giving teacher certificates for one of the villager education programs that I am personally involved in. I oversee the business plan for this project.

My address to them was as follows:

"Dear brothers and sisters, GSM associates, government authorities, young women, and young men—all who are present at this conference:

I was, and remain, so happy to be part of this meeting. I love the Telugu language. It is the only language here I do not know, but I love the way it is pronounced and how it sounds. I wish I knew it; I am only a scholar of Sanskrit and Pali. Since I can speak other languages in this country, it is better for me today to speak to you in the English language, especially since I have the best interpreter on site.

I love this country. Even though I was not born here, my soul, my heart, and my mind feel as though I was. This country is my land, my country, and my holy land. Therefore, I am all too willing to do what I have to do, such as the hospital project, homes for the homeless, and the education project. I am spending my own funds to help our people here.

Yet, this village community (see map) is too small compared to other parts of the world. However, here is my book. The original copy is handsome-looking. I will sell it on different campuses and in the book marketing industry for $35 (approx. 1,600 Indian Rupees). Let us say one million copies are sold; then we will have more funds than we need to accomplish our project.

It is not only I who can do that, but you, as the locals here, must give your hands, time, and heart. Together we can do it. As the U.S. President Reagan said, together we can make it. We will make the entire world know us—from the smallest villager to what we achieved—and inform our fellow men and women via my book. The world will know and give us support.

So, let us pray and be positive in thought with our mighty God. Let everything be in the hand of our God, not us. We, and only we alone, will not ever get the job done; but He guides us and orders us to do it, and that job will be done in His own way."

My wife noted that this kind of project is similar to what she is doing in America. I then let my wife take over (everyone stood up and clapped their hands so loudly for me and my wife).

My wife introduced herself and said she was so happy about this trip. She expressed that it was a special trip for her and that she was happy to be part of the educational project her husband started to train teachers.

"I always support my husband," she said, "because he is taking orders from the Almighty God, not himself. Even now, we are financing our own home to complete the project that was called to be done. I enjoyed seeing all the teachers, government workers, and GSM associated partners here today. You have such strong faith in Christ and have such beautiful dress. Keep going, doing what you are doing with the support of God, my husband, and the government of India. The job will be done."

We had to leave because our daughter was worried about where we were. We took her for a late luncheon. Thank you, and God bless you, and bye for now.

With cheerful eyes and clapping hands, we left the meeting happily. We took our daughter to the gulf and the beach and ate there with our driver, then returned to the hotel and took a nap.

November 30, 2004 8:05 AM

This is a record of my previous trip to India in 2003.

As soon as I completed my mission in Northern Thailand and Burma, I fulfilled a promise to my dear friend. We promised to work together to help our followers and our community in the nation, as well as internationally. Of course, I was doing my personal family duty as usually expected of me, and it was time for me to leave for India.

I took the airline to Chennai to meet my dear friend, Dr. Yesu. I had felt lost when he was in America as a member of GSM and the Mission of God as a whole. We have similar ideals and exchanged such pure and innocent ideas regarding Buddhism and Christianity. He took us together as a brotherhood.

Way before this trip, I was a student and teacher in India. I was happy there because I had been lost, with no direction, living in what seemed like accidental conditions. But through the wisdom that God gave me, it was beyond any academic work. I was taken from there to live my life, hiding at the hermitage. The Thai government thought I was dead because I had excommunicated myself from them.

I met too many kinds of people from around the world. We spoke in different languages and shared many thoughts, but in the end, we were bonding with the world and wanted something sincere and better. We were vegetarians; we thought we could eat simply to live. We shared what each of us had for eating and shared our journey around the Himalayan hillside.

Most of them said, "Hey Daney, you must teach us palmistry and astrology. You are the man who can show us the way; we are lost."

I said, "I am lost too. You are nuts! I am not any holy boy, but a happy Thai."

One girl from Japan felt close to me and expressed her love. I was so scared and ran away from her. Again and again, similar situations kept repeatedly happening. Later, there was a German girl; she said she saw something special in me and wanted to spend the rest of her life with me. She asked me to meditate on it and reply. Again, I had to escape. Here I was, scared of nothing, yet afraid of falling in love, not even knowing myself what love meant to me. We called ourselves friends daily, sharing everything we had, but I felt that I was just one of the Hippie group with no romantic love involved.

Anyway, those thoughts aside—you know I love India. Why? Because it is the motherland of the Thai cultural set. I feel I owe something to my motherland, God's work, and Buddha's teachings. My dream was seeking, then inward learning.

Dr. Yesu saw me and hailed a taxi to take me to a small home called the Salvation Army. He was so happy to see me. He asked me if my name appeared in the book record of the Salvation Army. I smiled and kept my secret.

I took a cold shower and hurried up as he had a train to catch (perhaps to Kakinada). Before I took the train, in the lateness of that night, I saw all of the poorest and oldest people, both men and young gangs. I felt so bad. I said, "Hey, one dollar is 60 Rupees. Why don't I give them away for their food?"

I gave them out one by one, and they followed me and told me, "God Bless you, Guru."

"Oh, I am not the Guru," I said, "but I give my life and my sympathy to them."

The newspapers, such as the *Indian Express*, said, "Foreign Guru gives million rupees to the homeless." Another news paper said, "The kindly man from the USA, who was Thailand-born, following the paths of God and Buddha, gave a million rupees away." Whatever they stated in the newspaper, I was careless about the fame, because I am who I am. I believe in that.

As soon as we arrived, I told Dr. Yesu's town. There were Brahmins and Hindus (see in my book) there to pick us up after 13 hours of a train drive. They gave the nicest, warmest welcome and put me in the most beautiful retreat. A Hindu man checked me into his friend's largest hotel in town.

The owner came over and said, "Welcome. I saw your picture in the news. It is a blessing to have you in here. Welcome to our town. If there is anything you want me to do, please say so."

The Indian man, the owner of the large hotel, continued, saying he knew I was building a hospital and homes for homeless children in the village (see the map). He said he was so impressed. "You are not even Indian, why do you do this?"

I said, "Yes, I am Indian, and this is my land and my Holy Land." He nodded and said "Namaste" to me.

Next, I was taken to the village. My picture was there; tons of crowds were there. They were so thankful to see me in person. They were so happy, blessing me and thankful to me that I was the key man to do the necessary project for them. I know that it was not my intentionality, but **HIS**.

My Address to Them:

"My name is Daney Dumdeang. I was here at the border years ago. I wished to keep coming all year and quite often. Three years ago, my wife and I just about made it. When we were in Singapore, I bought the airline ticket. We were just about in the air when we got a call saying the flight was canceled. My wife's heart was pumping when she heard that we got to go to India, and after the flight was canceled, we both sat in silence. We did not make it then. Now I am here without my wife."

The crowd said, "Please bring her next time."

I said, "Yes, I promise I will bring her." They asked me to stay in their house next time. I told them that although they are poor economically, they are the richest in the faith of God. They were so happy, standing firm.

I continued my talk, stating that I was called to be here and promised to complete the hospital based on **His** authority, not mine. I am taking this as accountability and could not help but continue His Mission because His spirit tells me to. The cry of God mingled with the cry of the people.

All are calling for action. I begged God for years that He would never stop me serving Him, and let Him pinpoint and guide me in what to do.

Here I am, participating as a partner with Him. I saw the haunting look on millions of faces—kept up and down—and I pray that I am not indifferent to them. I reflected on the great mission of such people as Mother Teresa.

Who am I? I often asked myself when I was younger; "I am the man of God, or I am his servant." What and why did He do what He did to me and my fellow man? With my own eyes, I see brothers as He sees them; an ideal entering my mind and my heart, sent from Him.

The Word must come forth. I believe you will understand the lone lines that call you into greater love. Why? I am here to respond to your needs. With my associated GSM and partnership with God, I will continue to complete the project for our community and for you all. I must stop my speaking now since I am tired from a long trip, but I will see you next speech tomorrow.

November 29, 2004 8:02 AM

Behold the Christ

I behold the Christ in you today. I would like to explore my thought that we have Christ, along with a quotation. One of the most difficult things we may have to do is look at others who appear different.

Yet, we can learn to look past differences when we learn to look for and **behold the Christ in everyone**.

No matter how different others may seem to be, we remember that everyone was created by God, and therefore everyone is created good. We do not need to understand or ever approve of the actions of others in order to behold the Christ in them. All we need is a willingness and a desire to bless others in our prayers.

Let us affirm: *I behold the everything that makes you unique. I love and acknowledge that our differences are the things that make us unique. I love and appreciate you. I behold the Christ in you now and always.*

I quote: *"Love the Lord your God with all your heart. Love your neighbor as yourself." Matthew 22:37, 39*

I would like to touch into the service of Dedication. The concluding act of the Christian drama of salvation is a great page of **Offering**. There is a double action here which is nevertheless a single movement. The prayers are presenting themselves unto God.

All they value, all they possess.

Yet marching into the **LIFE** of the world for responsible involvement.

Saturday, Nov 27, 2004 11:54 PM

My Thought on Patience

I am patient, for I know that God always answers my prayers. I relax and let go of concern about the "When" or "How" of answers to my prayers.

No matter how urgent my need seems to be (just like what occurred last Friday between the devilish inspector of the City and my workers; I have to slow down if I listen to my angel daughter, but I am who I am—He creates me for Who He Is, and He wants work for Him, so I got that done that day.

His assistance in my patience and His guard), I remember that most needs change but that **God's help is constant**.

God is the source of all knowledge, and divine understanding is available to me whenever I need it. When I rely on God's light and love, my eyes are open to **TRUTH** and my thinking becomes clear. With God's help, I take right action.

I quote: *"O the depth of the riches both of the wisdom and knowledge of God!" Romans 11:33*

Harmony

After my spiritual angel daughter told me, "Papa, how about making Thanksgiving Day a miracle?" Here is my mind's Harmony. It is not my angel daughter's word but must be from **HIM** via my angel daughter. So, I am willing to be a harmonious, loving person in all my relationships.

Whether we are following a blueprint of a house or a dish, we know that the right materials or ingredients are essential for a successful outcome. This is why, in order to live, work, or be in harmony with others, we need to include all the right ingredients in our relationships with them.

The good news is that God has already supplied us with the ingredients we need for harmonious, loving relationships.

We start with a heaping measure of love, given for the joy of loving, not for getting something in return. We include a generous portion of **Faith**—faith in God working through us. We add a pinch of patience to allow the very best results to come about. We stir in appreciation, also, for the Spirit of God that is within each person at all times.

I ask, believe, and act with the understanding that my prayers are being answered. The result is the kind of spiritual growth that is indeed true peace and joy.

My deepest desires are part of God's loving plan for me, and my faith lights the way to a better understanding of what that plan is. Placing my trust in the transforming power of faith, I do the best that I can at my daily tasks. Patiently I wait (just as Buddha taught me that he can wait, he can fast, he can think on the sands; so do I). I wait for God's answer and enjoy the bountiful gifts of this day.

Thanks be to God.

"Thou wilt keep him in perfect peace, whose mind is stayed on thee: because he trusteth in thee." — Isaiah 26:3

November 27, 2004 3:44 AM

Where is our heart in the sense of Christian meaning?

My heart and mind are touched by the wisdom of God.

I take right action.

Guidance

Am I experiencing the kind of problem where I feel defeated even before I begin searching for an answer? Perhaps the situation calls for more understanding, such as the housing repair situation at my property in the Northeast, caused by a city worker with an unethical mind.

The answers to this question, and all others, come by turning to God in prayer so that my heart and my mind are aligned with divine intelligence. As a beloved child of God, I am an heir to divine light. I open my mind and my heart to divine light. I am growing in awareness of what is right for me.

I quote: *"For he is our peace, who has made both one." Ephesians 2:14.*

I am willing to continue more on faith and harmony later on in a suitable chapter.

November 25, 2004 1:25 AM - Thanksgiving Day

Philosophical Reflections on Worship

I would like to ask you to acknowledge an earlier thought. It is a popular philosophical thought that has influenced Christian worshippers in the deepest sense. It is an abstract idea for those who want to be free from suffering; therefore, worshippers need God, and they depend on God alone.

I will state that these ideas were influenced by **Leibniz** or **Descartes**. They thought of worship where they divided substance into monads, numerology, and plurality. For the worshipper, then, each has a different individual substance which I would like to describe as being predicated.

To some extent, when a worshipper has an individual substance, it may be alike or different only numerically. I mean that the differences are understood in figures. For example, the substance of which all empirical things are composed—I will use the idea called by Leibniz "Monads." Worshippers then carried such ideas from their corporal things, which have certain characteristics known as plurality, quality, extension, and motivation (movability/flexibility).

Worshippers have not realized that substance is **INDEPENDENT** in respect to creation. Any substance exists only through creation and commences through annihilation or diminishes through natural means. Although these frequently transform into numbers of substances, they neither augment nor diminish. I will call this its **INTERNAL NATURE**.

For worship seeks the internal nature of substance. They need to conceive it by the mind, and the mind must be purified and free from those thoughts of created substance.

To me, as my mind clearly thinks to share with readers here: Between God and the creation of substance, the creation of substance is like an entire world and a mirror of God. The worshipper is struggling with the cause of an idea, and it must have as much reality (substance) as the idea represents—the final cause and efficient cause proposition.

Here, then, the worshippers get caught in the relationship among types of substance, namely mentality and different kinds of substances which extend the worshipper's mind to have a relationship to God (ethical or causality). The distinction here is that the worshipper thinks that God produces different substances according to different views. Since God has the world (or His creation, which I call the Internal Nature of God), the appropriate nature of each substance corresponds to what is happening to all others without, however, their acting upon one another directly.

I would like to theorize on the problems of worshippers on all these points. I feel they are based on a rival system that leads to skepticism (readers must keep this in mind for the last chapter). The reason being, I will conclude that there are external material things—matter consisting of primary qualities—which have an extended, distinct, and independent existence from their being perceived.

What is perception to worshippers? These are everything we perceive that cannot exist otherwise than in the worshippers' minds where they perceive them. What do we perceive beside our own ideas and sensations? Furthermore, the real problem worshippers have is that the ideal of perception leads them to believe in it; since they believe in it, it is impossible for worshippers to have knowledge of this matter distinct from perception or the **MIND**. Why? Because all perception has its **FOUNDATION** in the mind.

I know that the worshippers think of nothing more than an idea of their own mind and therefore cannot exist outside perception. Here is the real problem of the worshipper: they cannot miss perception if they reflect on what passes within their own mind, and the ideas of sensation or material matter are nothing more than what has passed within their minds.

Note: See my lecture for Winter Quarter 1972. Therefore, I should consult these concepts of ideas more in my notes in the same quarter, Green Book.

In the next session, I would add here regarding the world and its sufferings of the mind—that is where worshippers need a Savior. The notion of depending is upon God only.

Conclusion on the Act of Worship

I would like to emphasize that the worshipper's **ACT of devotion** is the presentation of the offering. Here, these worshippers are again offering up themselves in offering **UNTO GOD** their worldly possessions. It is an offering that is made, not a collection which is taken.

One must be aware that what is given is but a token indication that all of our goods are gifts to use in responsible living in the world.

At the close of the procession, a prayer of dedication is made, signifying that this action is intended for God's glory and the service of the neighbor. At this time and point, the prayers break forth into a doxology or hymn of praise to God the Father, Son, and Holy Spirit, which is a fitting finale to Act Two and the whole drama of salvation.

Act Three is the dramatic enactment of life in the Holy Spirit. It is a life of utter dependence upon God and utter responsibility for the world—a gift to all who rejoice in the Lord through the forgiveness of their sins.

After the epilogue, which may consist of a hymn which once again indicates and honors the God we stand before, plus a benediction, the actors leave with repentance, thankful praise, and creative love.

One day—tomorrow perhaps—they will return to rehearse again the drama of their Salvation so that they may remember who and whose they **ARE**.

November 24, 2004 Morning

I would like to further point out for my brothers and sisters who read this session: realize that the worshippers are here offering up themselves to God by placing the world in His hands. They are offering up themselves in presenting to God their responsibility in and for the world.

In brief, then, the Prayers, having received themselves and the world as **GIFTS** from God, are offering them back again.

Let us be precisely aware that prayers are made for the church, and then for the home, the state, and finally, economic life. It includes educational institutions and international structures.

The worshippers then turn with particular concern for those living at the far edge, forced out of this natural order. Intercessions are now offered for the poor and hungry (it is easy and obvious to see many priests refer to these), the sick and those in prison, for the outcast and those who have lost the kindly light of reason, and those who are on beds of death. In this action, the community is boldly involving itself in life and daringly entering into the existence of other creatures.

Further, I would like to point it out again:

The first scene begins with acts of petition and supplication. The prayers are not engaged in the manipulation of cosmic power, but rather they are surrendering into God's hands their future and destiny. The worshippers have turned their daily care over to the One Wise Forgiving Presence who is everywhere, and precisely here in the **DARKNESS of the UNKNOWN**.

November 26, 2004 - After Thanksgiving

A Reflection on Thanksgiving and Hunger

We are American people who celebrated our survival from death by hunger. The Native Indian people taught us how to eat, live, and survive. Now everyone celebrates that, including the writer myself.

But can we think of the rest of the world who are hungry, who have no refrigerator, no food, no money to buy anything to feed themselves nor their family? We eat here one meal that equates to one week or a month of food for the rest of the world, such as the poorest of the poor people in Thailand or India. It is so hard for us at home to think in the practical reality of sharing with human beings on earth.

I feel we, as Americans, are the super selfish ones on earth. We are hunting for imperialism and capitalism for super world power, but care only for ourselves, careless for the rest of the world. I am so super disappointed. This is why every Thanksgiving Day everyone enjoys so much at the dinner table, but not me.

How many billions of turkeys were killed for a day of just human desire and enjoyment? Can you think of stopping killing turkeys? They are our animal friends and they want to live their lives as much as us.

Look at the World Hunger Belt and Empires of History.

Let us examine how many people hunger in the world. In studying the history of nations, I have discovered an amazing fact—the power belt historically of the nations lies in the middle of the world. Look at the drawing in Appendix C and readers will see what I mean.

Chapter 2

INNER PEACE

After a real, total legal battle with an unethical business partner with whom I had conducted business for over ten years, I was so frustrated. He mocked my wife and my English pronunciation and claimed he was doing nothing wrong—completely different from what his people did to us. This caused my trip to be cut short, forcing me to return urgently from Thailand to continue the business relationship with him and his people.

He was liable to do more work but broke his promises. My plumbing was not done, nor did he do anything to help my tenants begin using the property. To me, what is lawful and what is illegal became a confusing nonsense. If I had no peace of mind—no Inner Peace—I would have continued to fight and state that my people did not do anything wrong, as long as it satisfied my tenants and me. But that counts for nothing when my "enemy-friend" has no judge but himself.

It is most frustrating and disturbing to deal with a dishonorable business company that makes many mistakes and claims that neither he nor his people did anything wrong, trying to brush it off as a "big timer." Whatever he said, he meant less. Well, enough is enough.

My heart told me so; my mind is touched by God. I am peaceful and secure. I radiate to the world when I am at peace in my mind and heart. I begin to feel at peace when I allow God to ask in and through me, when I allow divine love to fill me with peace.

Inner peace is not something that can be forced. I experience inner peace only when I relax and let God's love fill me through and through. Touched by the love of God, I know that God and I are one, and that all is well in my world.

I can maintain this sense of peace and well-being regardless of events. When chaos appears, when a situation seems to speak of anything but peace, I **FOCUS** on the potential for peace in every situation. I bless all involved and know that God's Love and Order are at work to bless and promote spiritual growth.

"Peace I leave with you, my peace I give unto you." — John 14:27

December 2, 2004

Faith

I got a call from one of my contractor companies saying there was bad news. I sat in silence. I asked, "What problem? What else bad news am I going to hear?"

He said, "Do not worry, everything must be fine. Please meet me next week or so."

I then fused with the question: *Why?* Is bad karma returning back to me? Well, let it call me. I have faith in **HIM** in my heart and myself.

My strong faith in God keeps me centered and ready for right action. Fear can render us incapable of creative thinking or right action only if we let it. Instead of reacting with fear when we hear disturbing news, let us meet such reports with instant, steadfast **FAITH**.

The Power of God is mighty to adjust, harmonize, heal, and inspire. Our steadfast faith in God assists us to turn from fearful thoughts to a deep respect for the power of God at work to bring forth good. We give thanks that good judgment and right action prevail and fortify us.

We become more optimistic because we know that God is good, and good is the only power there is. We are centered and ready to take right action at the right time; our strong faith always sees us through.

"I fear no evil; for thou art with me." — Psalm 23:4

December 3, 2004

There is nothing greater than the protection of God. The presence of God is active in my life, and I am protected.

No matter where I am, I live in the knowledge that God's presence is continually with me. God and I are one and cannot be separated. Whether I am traveling to new places or staying in the comfort of my own home, I know that I am never alone.

My family and friends are never alone either. I release any anxieties about their well-being, for I know that they, too, are being divinely protected throughout the day and night.

Through prayer and my belief that all is well, I free my mind from anxiety or concern, and my way is clear to enjoy the day. The presence of God is active in my life and in the lives of my loved ones. We are protected.

"Every word of God proves he is a shield to those who take refuge in him." — Proverbs 30:5

Healing

I have had the hardest time in my life. My mother passed away, my sister disowned me, my prospective daughter-in-law excommunicated me.

. I didn't see my three grandchildren. I have huge problems with contractors in my business who do not listen to my orders financially, accusing me of big losses, and I lose face as a reliable Thai man, and so on continually.

I know that there are a lot of people who may have more problems and are suffering more than me. But for me now—business, family, Mission trip—everything has been postponed. Everything has caused me unheard-of suffering, from the death of my family members, death after death. My brother died a few years ago, and again my younger brother died, and my mother recently. How can I cope with this serious human suffering and human depression?

This is why I am writing this chapter on healing; it will help my readers as well as help me.

Perhaps at the very time I need healing the most, I feel that I lack the strength, faith, or understanding to be healed. I put aside all doubt and know that it is the life of **GOD** within that heals me. I remember that Jesus prayed before he healed one person or a whole crowd. So do I pray, realizing that prayer is an important part of my life and my healing process.

Jesus healed people of all kinds of diseases. People He touched physically were healed, but so were those whom He prayed for who were miles away. So do I pray, knowing I will be healed.

The life of God within moves through me, healing and restoring me. God-Life within my cells responds to my prayers of healing. I am healthy and strong.

"And all the crowd sought to touch him, for power came forth from him and healed them all." — *Luke 6:19*

December 6, 2004 4:48 AM

Indian Journey Trip

From the small airport in the valley full of many Indian mountains, the three of us had breakfast. I believed that our Indian companions ate some breakfast as well, but not me. I ordered iced coffee, but I never got what I wanted because I believe that in India, ice is so expensive, and no one ordered or drank the way a Thai man like me drinks. So I just let it pass and took it as a sign that they cannot comprehend what I really wanted. Maybe I am so picky in terms of drinking and eating habits because I have an ulcer, so I am so careful about what I am going to put in my stomach. I have experienced many of my friends eating dirty food in India and returning to America to get food poisoning and be sick for the rest of their lives. I was proud of my wife and daughter who ate well and complained about nothing regarding the food; they even knew the theme of the food better than me.

Here we checked into a small Great Bistis Jet from that town to Hyderabad. We got fed with Indian food. I requested vegetarian, but it was terrible looking, so I did not bother to look at it. I then kept asking for small and cute bottles of water. I took a few to the ground with me; I even took them to America with me because they are so small and easier to carry along in your pockets. The stewards were laughing at me for the way I kept asking for water.

We flew about an hour and a half; there were very beautiful Indian mountain views. I met an Indian engineer who lives in Hyderabad, and he gave me his card. He said one of his cousins is studying for an engineering degree at Wisconsin, so he may go and visit him soon. I also exchanged my card with him, and he said, "Next time, next trip, come over to the small town where we just left. There is a nice hotel and such a beautiful beach around the shore." That gentleman also recommended for us to go visit different places in Hyderabad, but my Indian friend said those places are far away and we would need to stay overnight and so forth.

Here we were landing on the ground. I prayed again: *Thanks God, we are saved by Him.*

After we checked out at Hyderabad, there was a man who introduced himself. "I am Yesu's brother." In our concept, we all thought that Yesu has a brother in Hyderabad. We all shook hands with him, and were pleased to meet him. Later we learned that means he is a "Brother in Christ."

He took us to look for a hotel. We tried the government hotel first, but it was full. Then we checked into the Ambassador Hotel. We opened three rooms—paid by me, of course. At the time we checked out, the manager said, "I will give you 50% off because I saw you in the *Indian Express* news and you are my new role model. I wish I had a big heart like you. Next trip when you come, you will get free of charge."

I said thank you so much. The day we checked out, it was such a surprise to my wife and Yesu that I got 50% off; they did not know why.

I thought Yesu paid for himself because he said he had already checked out. I then paid for myself, my wife, and my daughter. Later on, the manager said the room that Yesu lived in was not yet paid. Here we go again—laying off communication. I do not mind paying, but he must communicate with me. The Indian way is so confusing and indirect.

That day, my daughter asked if she could sleep in. We then went out to look at the view without our daughter. We went to the bank on and on to pay what Yesu claimed we owed about reimbursement of air tickets. Again, it was confusing. First we bought the ticket from the small town airport to New Delhi and Chennai, and we ran out of time, so I confirmed only the small airport town to Chennai. But the fun about it was that Yesu wanted to keep whatever arrangement. I just paid whatever indicated in the invoice; it seemed to make Yesu confused. He wrote a note for the travel agency to reimburse the rest of the money to him. He seemed happy with it.

I would like to describe the Hyderabad town a little bit. It is a larger town than Kakinada, very clean and modernized. Last time when I was alone, I took a bus and small taxi and I felt comfortable with my direction and where I went. I spent a lot of time sitting in the big park and saw poor Indian cleaner ladies. They used old-style brooms just like when I was a young boy; I used to have them and help my family to clean the farm and so forth. I enjoyed my reflection of my past.

This time we were taken by **Premaraja**—but of course, we paid for gas or whatever Yesu ordered to pay. This man, later on we learned, is the minister for the largest prison and he is a very active one. He has a nice wife and two children. He testified how he became a Christian (see his testimony).

The next day, my wife and daughter shopped for Indian clothing. My daughter bought what she wanted, two of them, and my wife bought some too. I kept drinking fresh sugarcane juice, and we went sightseeing to such places as the Taj Mahal and old Indian government halls full of historical buildings built by the British. There are full marble stones; they are so beautiful (see our picture). My daughter also shopped for Indian herbal tea to bring to America. I shopped for nothing but one cute bag to carry my book and small belongings because that bag looked like something my mother used—that kind of style. When I brought it to America, Mother Betty loved it. I am glad that she loves it, so I right away gave it to her. She was so happy to have it.

At the hotel, my wife and daughter were getting great sleep, but I wrote my report and my book, as I usually do. I emailed my spiritual daughter about my business that she reported to me—that here is the urgent matter about property in the Northeast—so I released and authorized AMC to respond with my spiritual daughter. She has done very well. I am proud of her. If you know how to run business, you do not need to be there; you can operate your business around the world, and that is what I have done.

Here my wife and I went to visit a morning worship church in the center of downtown. The minister who spoke that day came from Jordan. He said he has known God many years ago and dreamed to be in India for such a long time. It reminds me of my wife's dream. He said as long as we have faith in Him, we get everything and He brings you to meet our needs. He is a white man from Jordan. We did not finish his second sermon because we needed to get our daughter and meet Yesu and get ready to go to the airport to catch our flight to Chennai.

What happened here at the airport was the flight was delayed three hours. So my daughter, Premaraja, and Yesu went out to go eat. Premaraja asked my daughter how much money I made in America and so forth, which made my daughter uncomfortable with those questions, which we learned later on.

I was so sick and plus upset with Yesu about his return schedule. We discussed that he could return to his town by train, which I would take care of his expenses. He did not book or reserve it; he said he needs to catch the plane back from Chennai. I was so hot then. I then gave him a look: "Okay, you are the director and so forth; you need to be clear and have some kind of certain plan and certain schedule, especially when you were working with me. I needed to know ahead of time. I hate surprises more than anything else in my life."

I informed him that a few strangers who listened to my conversation with him were so happy, more interested in me. Some went out of their way and bought me Indian coffee and said, "I saw you in the *Indian Express* news and read it and learned a lot of your strong intentionality to help our nation. You are special. I feel refreshingly spiritual when I just saw you. You are full of energy and big heart and enlighten us in your speech just like the former leader, Great Mahatma Gandhi."

I said, "I am not him, but I love what he did and who he is. I always look at him as my role model." Just like you, the conversation went on and on. I then took it easier. I believe my ulcer got into me. My wife went to get free Indian tea and split it for me. I took some medicine that I bought from America.

We took off by great jet airliner for another hour and a half and we took a taxi to the Salvation Army. I paid for the taxi and let my daughter sleep. We went to eat with Babu in an upper-class hotel and took some food back to our daughter. I paid every Rupee back to Yesu that he claimed I owned, etc. My wife found out a few things from the register—booked much real charge for the room, etc. She was so disappointed.

My daughter and I were at an internet place by tuk-tuk. We emailed friends and family and business as usual (mine anywhere, I do not know whom my daughter wrote to, that was her business, not mine). We took off from the Salvation Army. I met my Brahmin friend here and said goodbye to him. I missed him and he missed me. He said he was so happy that he met my wife and my daughter. "They are great people, you have such a great family, brother," said my Brahmin friend whom I have no doubting in, and whom I trust since day one since I met him years ago. We said goodbye sadly.

We brought three boxes of my book by my wife and my daughter. Thanks to them. We said goodbye to Yesu and Babu. We took Thai Airlines back to Bangkok. On the plane, my wife and my daughter slept most of the trip. I was writing the agenda of mission and engagement speaking in Bangkok. Here on the ground, saved by Him again. My spiritual author and her cousin were there for us and they called a taxi and we stayed at a dinner place. Nidnoi left with her cousin.

Next day we went to stay in Raja Hotel, which is closest to Peter's family. There again, my wife and my daughter turned in and slept. I was at the largest prison in Bangkok and gave a talk to refresh the spirituality of prisoners—over 5,000 of them. They realized that no matter where they are, they were free. After listening to my definition of freedom of choice and freedom to [act], they were happy. I felt full of energy.

Here there was a **Miracle** that occurred again. My daughter lost her passport and everything at the airport. The hotel tried everything to help, and she got her personal belongings thanks to the hotel management with mints and my book.

We missed my plane that day and we waited for the next day without penalty. Normally we have to pay a penalty up to $400, but the ground manager was so nice and waived everything. So I thanked her with my book and wrote a note in the book; she was so happy. I feel that my first book was sold for $400—that is the way I look at it.

Three of us were tired and enjoying ourselves at the same time; in other words, we had mixed feelings. My daughter had a hard time with her friend in America calling her late at night. I tried to write my agenda of speaking engagements and transfer it to notes, and also tried to think and give clearer thoughts to my fellow Indian friends. But my daughter on the phone was disturbing me so much.

But I dealt with it. Plus, on the street, she was so Western-style in an older-fashioned Indian country tradition. Millions of eyes of both young and old men concentrated on my daughter, which was bothering me too much. Even though I told her she must wear better, longer pants and so forth, she kept saying that she was hot and didn't want to dress up, etc.

Well, I said, either deal with the eyes of those men or deal with your wearing style—one or the other. Another thing, she kept ordering stupid Indian tea, drink after drink with my wife. They enjoyed drinking stupid Indian tea, and the boy kept coming to knock on the door almost every 30 minutes because my daughter loves that stupid tea. But I do not. I love the banana and some fruit when they gave or served us in our room.

Sometimes my wife and I bought some fruit from outside. Even when we did not need to, we just helped the poor sellers. They often didn't have any change, even for 100 Rupees. We felt bad, so we gave the money away without taking their fruit.

I visited a Christian mission operation hall next to the hotel where we were staying. I introduced myself as the mission man from Thailand and America. They were so happy to have me there. I returned back a few times; they were so happy.

Besides visiting different religious affairs, I also kept emailing Maria and my children in Thailand, my special author cousins, and so forth. Of course, I had some business to do here. So I made a lot of emails to intended businessmen around my hotel. They were nicest to me and adopted me as "Papa" and told me to visit them and share their lives with me. They told me next time I come to India, just stay with them and take them along to America.

I feel so bad to see them have such a hard life to live in that part of the world. Yet, on the other hand, they have the richest customs and traditions. They are the root of cultural custom where the most excellent thought of our ancestors follows the world, such as Hindu religious thought and Buddhism. And how about the symbolism of love from the husband to the wife? The King loved his wife and built the most popular hall, called the **Taj Mahal**. That man showed how strong love is for mankind—an example for us around the world.

Yes, there are the poorest people in the world here, but they have the richest tradition in the world. So with only spirit and peace in their hearts and minds, they can cope with society from day to day. And their life is full of peace. I am proud of them.

It was shocking to me to see one group of Hindu men at the bar, drunk, looking at my daughter and misunderstanding that I had a young working woman with me. We stopped at that place because we needed something (my daughter wanted to buy whisky). When the price was so high, my daughter wanted to walk away. I do not understand what they said to hurt us in the Hindi language. We did not buy. One ugly, fat-looking guy came over to my face and exchanged words with me. I said, "If you give an Indian price, I buy now; otherwise, get out of my face."

He then ordered the owner to sell to us. It tasted yucky—the worst whisky in the world. You never, ever expect to buy good beer or any whisky in India. They have the worst taste in the world. Why? Because most Hindu people did not drink, so therefore they did not know how to make alcohol. Period. We bought it and went back to the hotel. We drank it and threw away the rest of the leftovers because it was a terrible, terrible taste of whisky.

It was impressive and irritating at the same time in my heart that most of the workers of the richest hotel there loved to go out with my daughter. They kept leaving their phone numbers and addresses in my room for my daughter. One man even went out of his way to buy a brand new scooter and told my daughter that now we can go out and he can show my daughter the city with the brand new scooter. I kind of laughed and was shocked at what those people were thinking.

We did some small shopping here in Kakinada. Our friends thought they were helpful and took us, for instance, to buy eyeglasses that had fancy cases we did not need; we needed prescription glasses. We finally gave up letting him help us. This is not a problem only in India, but in Thailand and most of Southeast Asia—because they think they are helpful, but they control us and want us to do things their way. They did not ever understand our Western thought or Western lifestyle, or our routine of daily action or shopping from day to day, because they never lived in our society in the Western world. Therefore, they are helpless instead of helpful. So I was so, so disappointed. Just reminding my Westerners that we must be aware of the real face of the East in that way.

I am glad that I am living and dealing with a multicultural society, and I taught in too many school districts here in Oregon and around the Northwest. I am glad for what I did for my Western or American followers.

My books were taken by my Brahmin friend, Mr. P. R., to Chennai. My impression was that he just did it for me, but I learned that he had to go to see his daughter at Chennai anyway. After I met him at the Salvation Army, we wanted to take him for a veggie dinner. He said he had his daughter cook dinner for him and he needed to hurry up and see his daughter and have dinner with her.

In my entire life, I was so dummy; I never questioned that a Brahmin can have a wife. I said, "I thought you were Brahmin and you cannot have a wife."

He said, "Oh no, just like you. But I am Brahmin. I can marry and have a family."

I said that I was glad. I did not know that before at all. He kept smiling at me.

My daughter started getting scared of the Indian train and people peeping over in her cloth. Plus, in Rupees—those Rupees were given as the tip for hotel boys. Now I feel bad; hotel boys must think that these small Rupee-tipping Westerners like us must hate them or get back at them with something. I hope he will not keep smiling at **Dona's** "pee-pee" forever. I feel terrible. Later, I clarified with my wife why they were irritated to give a tip to the hotel boy; I thought they did not know the custom. So I demanded, "Please give a tip to the boys." They did eventually. Now I have a funny and sad "pee-pee" story of Dona up to Thanksgiving Day in late November 25, 2004. Dona seemed to enjoy telling the story to her cousin Sara and her Grandma Dorothy. I asked my wife if Dona was drunk on Thanksgiving Day because she was so excited about her "Pee-pee" storyteller.

Because of her fear of taking the long, long train to Chennai, we (I make the decision most of the time because I have to comfort my daughter; I do not want her to suffer—money is not important to me, I could do it just for my daughter) arranged with a driver to take us to a small airport where it took 4 and a half hours to drive. We got up at 2 AM in the middle of the night and started driving on the road.

It seems my friend and driver did not know his way because he never did it before. My friend is so poor and lives in the poor style, but is rich in the spirit. We got to the airport, but before we got there, my friend again never ever asked us one single word: "Do you want to eat or drink?"

He stopped at the most ugly, stinky, and yucky place in the world. The cook had hand disease; the wife did not wash her hands to cook some kind of Roti for my wife, my daughter, my friend, and my driver. I was so polite, so I said I am not hungry but I can have hot water. My friend said, "Please, please eat and drink." I said, "No, no, no." He did not understand at all. I could not even sit down. Why? Because a million flies flew around me, in my eyes, in my mouth, in my nose, etc. But I was proud of both my wife and my daughter that they could cope with that, but not me.

I told my friend I am going for a walk and to take Hindu temple-looking pictures with my driver. Here hundreds of chickens were taken by an Indian seller by bicycle. The chickens kept crying and crying for their lives. I said this is sad. Why do they take chickens to sell and kill them for our survival, for our being? Can we eat veggie and not kill our animal friends, including chickens?

I was down and sad. I told the seller, "Can you change jobs and do something rather than terrifying these chickens and selling them and killing them? They are alive and they have lives."

Full of tears, he said, "My master, I will give up what I am doing. I can be cleaner and do something else and it will make me feel better," said the Indian chicken seller. And he nodded at me and said, "You are my **GURU**. I never wanted to hear from anyone before, but somehow my heart told me to listen to you. I saw the ray in you, sir."

Said that man, we said "Namaste" and left one another.

My friend said, "Let's go catch the plane." As soon as we got there, we learned that the plane was delayed three more hours. And the door of the airport had not yet opened. So we took some pictures of the small airport and we gave 10,000 Rupees back for our driver. Again, my friend never told us ahead of time. It is most frustrating, **IS IT NOT?**

Here we are in the small car with the best driver—I trust him, he is good—I called him **BUBU**. Maybe that is the common name called in India.

My wife, my daughter, and my friend were sleeping in the car. Only my driver and I were awake. I saw a smiling face, a happy, dignified lady in my spiritual body. I said, "Who are you?"

She said, **"I am Mother Teresa."**

"Son, I came to you to thank you for the continuation of my mission. I have done my share of my life. No one I trust to continue to do my will and my plan but you. Please do not become discouraged with the situation happening to you. Do not do it for one person who is not fair or who dishonors you, but you do according to **HIS** Order, just like He ordered me from my so-called country in South America to be here. Now physically I am leaving my work, but He appointed you to continue my work as if it is His work. So thanks, and be healthy and full of energy and go on doing what you are doing. I am behind you. If you need me, just sit tight and call my name."

I said, "Okay, Mother, I am your spiritual son. I am taking care of your will and your incompleteness of mission. Please do not worry. I am clear and knowing myself; I am the man of my word. And please realize that what you did is not only for Indian people but for people in the entire world, and they honor you until the end of the earth."

She hugged me and gave me a big smile and disappeared. I took note then (see in my wife's white paper note).

Today is Saturday

I was so struggling in my decision and so worried about my operation, the way things go. I felt that my decision on business was unlearned and made a little weak business sense, the way my spiritual author emailed me and told me my characteristics and the way I run the ship. I was down so I kept reading the Bible below: **God loves me and is with me always.**

I am a beloved child of God, and God's love guides and nurtures me, loving me as I am, not for what I have done or will do. God wants only good for me.

I give thanks for God's love and show my appreciation for it by expressing unconditional love to others. I do not hold grudges, but rather forgive freely and completely. I bless everyone around me and radiate love, and that love is returned to me a hundred times over. God's love is constant at all times, in all places and circumstances. Though seasons change and people change and the events of my life change from day to day, God never does.

God's Love is the secure foundation on which I build my life, and I know that this foundation will uphold me and support me now and always.

"Love never ends." — 1 Corinthians 13:8

Tomorrow I'll point it out more in a later chapter

December 6, 2004 5:53 AM

Today I was up earlier as usual. I am doing routine office work, mediating, and writing one chapter.

After I have had a hard time dealing with too many problems with my life—i.e. business, family relationships, etc.—there are too, too overwhelming things and many frustrations to cope with. My wife is super busy with her studies. I am so busy with business, dealing with old and young clients and so forth.

My closest friend came with her problem while I was lying down for a nap. I believe I got a real, real bad cold. She told me that she was fired from her Thai restaurant job even though she did call at work, plus she got paid short. I listened carefully and I did call the place where she worked, introduced myself whom I am. Then the old former friend, a business friend over 30 years ago, returned my call and tried to solve the problem. He apologized for what happened and he didn't know that Paida is my closest friend whom I assigned to work there.

He will meet sometime at the restaurant this coming Tuesday. He was on the phone saying he helped a lot of people—Thai, Lao, etc. I said, "Well, they help you too. There are always two ways; they are your employees, you are their employer."

I myself helped a lot of people too and I didn't expect anything from their return. I just voluntarily help on and on. Said he even wears broken jeans. I said I even wear dirty clothes daily and work with all my clients. These are outside of our internal peace. We have to be honorable and doing what our soul told us to do. We cannot just take any advantage from anyone, especially here in the foreign land in America. And this is why I stepped in and helped my people, okay.

Ending up with an agreement and ending the phone call. I went to church with my wife even though I was so busy. But it is nice to go to church with her and see my followers at the church. Even though I stopped by to collect rent at Plum Street and went for my appointment at Milwaukee, so my mind is so, so occupied. However, the minister says the great thing as such: **We must Repent.**

Return Yourself to Basic Work and Work with God

I am today reading back to basics: **Romans 12:9-13**. It states that the disciple of Christian life [must act with love]. To discipline ourselves is to know that we need to seek help and advice when problems arise, just like today's problem.

This discipline holds true in our spiritual journey: talking with friends and sharing problems and joys makes both of us grow spiritually. Just as beginning our day with our friends and exercise improves our lives physically, so the time we spend devotionally strengthens us spiritually.

Prayer: We give you thanks, dear Heavenly Father, for each day of our lives and the opportunities and joys each day brings for doing Your will. Amen.

Thanks for the Day, Taking time for God brings strength for living. *(Catherine J. Gould, New York)*

I quoted her Prayer Focus: **THOSE NEEDING ENCOURAGEMENT.** Furthermore, after I emailed my spiritual daughter, knowing myself better, my mind is opening to the **TRUTH**.

Open and Receptive

My mind is open to the **TRUTH**, and my life is enriched by spiritual vision. I no longer feel confused or uncertain. Clear, true ideas flow into my mind. I see evidence of the truth whenever I look.

My heart is receptive to all the love, all the blessings that come to me. I am in tune with good, and I feel my oneness with God, my oneness with all life. With an open mind and receptive heart, I put on the Christ nature.

I am no longer the same person I was even a moment ago. I am a new person in Christ, and miracles are happening through me. I think anew. Renewed faith fills my heart. I am a witness to the wonder happening in everyday life. I am able to comprehend that miracles are taking place in me, through me, and all around me.

"Be renewed in the spirit of your minds, and put on the new nature." — Ephesians 4:23-24

Chapter 3
THE CRISIS OF FAITH

By Dr. Sompong Daney Dumdeang

When we speak of a "Crisis of Faith," to me—as a writer, author, and co-author of a number of books in many languages—I mean something different from a crisis in morals, such as reliability or loyalty, or a crisis in political ideology or respect for the law. In fact, I even mean something other than a crisis in religion—neither in Buddhism, nor Christianity, nor Hinduism, nor other religions.

For in all these instances, the crisis is one of **HUMAN** attitude and character. It is concerned with the problem of a practical age or generation—that is, with sociological phenomena.

Although faith is connected with morality and religion, and is always a human attitude, it is nevertheless differentiated from them by being a particular faith: **Faith in an agentless something beyond mankind.**

Appendix I: The Personal Crisis

(This is a special appendix containing my situation with my younger sister. However, I am certain that it is going to be beneficial for all readers as well.)

I am bothered by my younger sister, whom I have helped so much, just as I promised my father I would do. My father said, "If something was to happen to me, please take care of the youngest child." This is my youngest sister.

I said to my papa, "Please do not worry! I promise and I will keep my promise and will do my best for you."

I took care of her even more than my own daughter. I did not even know who she really was or if she really is my sister because I never grew up with her. I was in India and Northern Thailand, busy with my passion, my preaching, and my mission in both Christianity and Buddhism. Plus, I was involved deeply with UNESCO and UNICEF. I never knew her until the first time I actually met her when she was six or seven years old.

I asked if her dad was still a drunk as usual. I thought to myself, *Is she my sister's daughter or my niece?*

She had a sad face and was mad at me the day we met because, in her mind, she told herself that I was her father. She asked me, "What do you mean *your* dad? My dad is *your* dad?" She must have thought I was being mean to her. She was so negative with me since day one when we met.

I knew who she really was. I was here in the U.S.A. and she graduated from university in Thailand. I brought her here and took care of her even way before that. I always sent money to support her while she was doing undergraduate work there.

I thought we were getting closer together. One day she interviewed me, and she learned about what kind of life I was going through. She became aware of me as a man who is her blood brother and her biological relation—not just the man who is an American living the American lifestyle. She said, "Now I know my brother so well. I will write the history of my brother. Now I have discovered my brother as a real person, and he is my brother."

As time passed, my mother passed away. My sister was financially suffering. With her poverty, she got lost. She is no longer close to me or trying to have a noble, functional family life. She disowned me. In an email, she stated, "You are not my brother and I am not your sister."

It has been hurting me badly until this moment. At my mother's funeral, I hugged her and I talked to her, but she was full of cold blood. I feel that something is wrong with her. I am trying and keep trying to forgive her, but it is so hard and so difficult. I pray daily and nightly, but it seems it is going nowhere.

February 28, 2005

I was up meditating and praying at 1:00 AM as usual after writing my chapter. I read and reread my manuscript and I thought: *What is forgiveness?*

The Way of Forgiveness

I am almost certain that we all have gone through family or human suffering at one time or another. We share this together. When family disowns you, you must learn and try to forgive him or her. Am I right?

In my case, I love and support my sister ethically and spiritually, and again, I love her dearly. Now that she has pronounced to the world that she disowns me, should I forgive her? Or should I let it go? Or should I let time be to see if that will ease the pain or if it is the answer for my pain?

We all say we want peace. Though few of us seem to know the way to peace, Jesus knows the way, though it is not always clear to us. We are generally unwilling to walk it. Jesus promises, however, to be with us and to show us His way through the conflicts that mire us.

I then thought further that there are two authors of *The Upper Room* who have addressed this issue. I am sure it may help me and my readers as well. I would like to summarize their thoughts:

In *The Way of Forgiveness*, **Marjorie Thompson** writes that forgiving requires that we name behaviors as inexcusable. But it also requires that we distinguish between the person and the **ACT**.

Author **Flora Slosson Wuellner** writes in *Forgiveness, the Passionate Journey*: "When we are victims of radical evil, we are not asked to forgive the evil act.

. We are asked to remember that the perpetrator, though trapped for now in evil, is nonetheless a child of God."

Jesus' prayer from the cross, *"Father, forgive them; for they know not what they do" Luke 23:34, KJV*, may sound as if Jesus was excusing His tormentors. But Jesus is not excusing them any more than He excused Judas' betrayal, ignored Peter's denial, or closed His eyes to the desertion of His followers.

Jesus' prayer from the cross was a redemptive exercise in remembering God. They were made in God's image and were children of God. They were capable of knowing and doing better.

*Jesus could have called them evil, **BUT** to do so would have been a dismissal of His life and death—that God gives up on no one. "While we were yet sinners, Christ died for us" Romans 5:8, NRSV.*

Forgiveness is the "narrow way" of which Jesus speaks *Luke 13:24,* a door we cannot enter without stooping. It is the only way through hate and fear to the promise of reconciliation and peace.

Chapter 4
YOU ARE ACCEPTED

"Moreover the law entered, that the offence might abound. But where sin abounded, grace did much more abound." — Romans 5:20

These words of Paul summarize his apostolic experience, his religious message as a whole, and the Christian understanding of life.

To discuss these words, or to make them the text of even several sermons, has always seemed impossible to me. I have never dared to use them before. But something has driven me to consider them during the past few months—a desire to witness to the two facts which appeared to me, in hours of retrospection, as the all-determining facts of our life: the abounding of **sin** and the greater abounding of **grace**.

There are few words more strange to most of us than "sin" and "grace". They are strange just because they are so well known. During the centuries, they have received distorting connotations and have lost so much of their genuine power that we must seriously ask ourselves whether we should use them at all, or whether we should discard them as useless tools.

But there is a mysterious fact about the great words of our religious tradition: they cannot be replaced. All attempts to make substitutions—including those I have tried myself—have failed to convey the reality that was to be expressed; they have led to shallow and impotent talk. There are no substitutions for words like "sin" and "grace".

But there is a way of rediscovering their meaning—the same way that leads us down into the depth of our human existence. In that depth, these words were conceived, and there they gained power for all ages. There they must be found again by each generation, and by each of us for himself. Let us, therefore, try to penetrate the deeper levels of our life in order to see whether we can discover in them the realities of which our text speaks.

The Meaning of Sin: Separation

Do the men of our time still have a feeling for the meaning of sin?. Do they, and do we, still realize that sin does not mean an immoral act? "Sin" should never be used in the plural. Not *our sins*, but rather **our sin** is the great, all-pervading problem of our life.

Do we all know that it is arrogant and erroneous to divide men into "sinners" and the "righteous"?. For by way of such a division, we can usually discover that we ourselves do not quite belong to the "sinners," since we have avoided heavy sins, have made some progress in the control of this or that sin, and have been humble enough not to call ourselves "righteous".

Are we still able to realize that this kind of thinking and feeling about sin is far removed from what the great religious tradition, both within and outside the Bible, has meant when it speaks of sin?.

I should like to suggest another word to you, not as a substitute for the word "sin," but as a useful clue in the interpretation of the word "sin": **Separation**.

Separation is an aspect of the experience of everyone. Perhaps the word "sin" has the same root as the word "asunder". In any case, sin is separation. To be in the state of sin is to be in the state of separation.

And separation is threefold:

1. There is separation among individual lives.

2. There is separation of a man from himself.

3. There is separation of all men from the Ground of Being.

This three-fold separation constitutes the state of everything that exists; it is a universal fact. It is the fate of every life. And it is our human fate in a very special sense.

We, as men, know that we are separated. We not only suffer with all other creatures because of the self-destructive consequences of our separation, but we also know *why* we suffer. We know that we are estranged from something to which we truly belong, and with which we should be united. We know that the fate of separation is not merely a natural event like a flash of sudden lightning, but that it is an experience in which we actively participate, in which our whole personality is involved, and that as fate, it is also guilt.

Separation which is fate and guilt constitutes the meaning of the word "sin". It is this which is the state of our entire existence, from its very beginning to its very end. Such separation is prepared in the mother's womb, and before that time, in every preceding generation. It is manifest in the special actions of our conscious life. It reaches beyond us into all the succeeding generations.

It is our existence itself. Existence is separation! Before sin is an act, it is a state.

The Meaning of Grace: Reunion

We can say the same things about grace. For sin and grace are bound to each other. We do not even have a knowledge of sin unless we have already experienced the unity of life, which is grace. And conversely, we could not grasp the meaning of grace without having experienced the separation of life, which is sin.

Grace is just as difficult to describe as sin.

- For some people, grace is the willingness of a divine king and father to forgive over and again the foolishness and weakness of his subjects and children. We must reject such a concept of grace; for it is merely a childish destruction of human dignity.

- For others, grace is a magic power in the dark places of the soul, but a power without any significance for practical life—a quickly vanishing and useless idea.

- For others, grace is the benevolence that we may find beside the cruelty and destructiveness in life. But then, it does not matter whether we say "life goes on," or whether we say "there is grace in life". If grace means no more than this, the word should and will disappear.

- For other people, grace indicates the gifts that one has received from nature or society, and the power to do good things with the help of those gifts.

But grace is more than gifts. In grace, something is overcome. Grace occurs "in spite of" something; grace occurs in spite of separation and estrangement.

Grace is the reunion of life with life, the reconciliation of the self with itself. Grace is the acceptance of that which is rejected. Grace transforms fate into a meaningful destiny; it changes guilt into confidence and courage. There is something triumphant in the word "grace": in spite of the abounding of sin, grace abounds much more.

The Struggle Between Separation and Reunion

And now let us look down into ourselves to discover there the struggle between separation and reunion, between sin and grace—in our relation to others, in our relation to ourselves, and in our relation to the Ground and Aim of our being. If our souls respond to the description that I intend to give, words like "sin" and "separation," "grace" and "reunion," may have a new meaning for us.

But the words themselves are not important. It is the response of the deepest levels of our being that is important. If such a response were to occur among us this moment, we could say that we have known grace.

Separation from Others Who has not, at some time, been lonely in the midst of a social event?. The feeling of our separation from the rest of life is most acute when we are surrounded by it in noise and talk. We realize then, much more than in moments of solitude, how strange we are to each other, how estranged life is from life.

Each one of us draws back into himself. We cannot penetrate the hidden center of another individual; nor can that individual pass beyond the shroud that covers our own being. Even the greatest love cannot break through the walls of the self. Who has not experienced that disillusionment of all great love?. If one were to hurl away his self in complete self-surrender, he would become a nothing, without form or strength, a self without self, merely an object of contempt and abuse.

Our generation knows more than the generation of our fathers about the hidden hostility in the ground of our souls. Today we know much about the pervasive aggressiveness in every being. Today we can confirm what Immanuel Kant, the prophet of human reason and dignity, was honest enough to say: there is something in the misfortune of our best friends which does not displease us. Who amongst us is dishonest enough to deny that this is true also of him?.

Are we not almost always ready to abuse everybody and everything, although often in a very refined way, for the pleasure of self-elevation, for an occasion for boasting, for a moment of lust?. To know that we are ready is to know the meaning of the separation of life from life, and of "sin abounding".

The most irrevocable expression of the separation of life from life today is the attitude of social groups within nations towards each other, and the attitude of nations themselves towards other nations. The walls of distance, in time and space, have been removed by technical progress, but the walls of estrangement between heart and heart have been incredibly strengthened.

The madness of the German Nazis and the cruelty of the lynching mobs in the South provide too easy an excuse for us to turn our thoughts from our own selves. But let us just consider ourselves and what we feel when we read, this morning and tonight, that in some sections of Europe all children under the age of three are sick and dying, or that in some sections of Asia millions without homes are freezing and starving to death.

The strangeness of life to life is evident in the strange fact that we can know all this, and yet can live today, this morning, tonight, as though we were completely ignorant. And I refer to the most sensitive people amongst us. In both mankind and nature, life is separated from life. Estrangement prevails among all things that live. Sin abounds.

Separation from Self It is important to remember that we are not merely separated from each other. For we are also separated from ourselves. *Man Against Himself* is not merely the title of a book, but rather also indicates the rediscovery of an age-old insight.

Man is split within himself. We like to condemn self-love; but what we really mean to condemn is contrary to self-love. It is that mixture of selfishness and self-hate that permanently pursues us, that prevents us from loving others, and that prohibits us from losing ourselves in the love with which we are eternally loved.

He who is able to love himself is able to love others also. He who has learned to overcome self-contempt has overcome his contempt of others. But the depth of our separation lies in just the fact that we are not capable of a great and merciful divine love towards ourselves. On the contrary, in each of us there is an instinct of self-destruction which is as strong as our instinct of self-preservation. In our tendency to abuse and destroy others, there is an open or hidden tendency to abuse and destroy ourselves. Cruelty towards others is always also cruelty towards ourselves. Nothing is more obvious than the split in both our unconscious life and conscious personality.

Without the help of modern psychology, Paul expressed the fact in his famous words: **"For I do not do the good I desire, but rather the evil that I do not desire."**. And then he continued in words that might well be the motto of all depth psychology: **"Now if I should do what I do not wish to do, it is not I that do it, but rather sin which dwells within me."**.

The Apostle sensed a split between his conscious will and his real will, between himself and something strange within and alien to him. He was estranged from himself; and that estrangement he called "sin". He also called it a strange "law in his limbs," an irresistible compulsion. How often we commit certain acts in perfect consciousness, yet with the shocking sense that we are being controlled by an alien power!. That is the experience of the separation of ourselves from ourselves, which is to say "sin," whether or not we like to use that word.

Separation from the Ground of Being Thus, the state of our whole life is estrangement from others and ourselves, because we are estranged from the Ground of our being, because we are estranged from the origin and aim of our life. And we do not know where we have come from, or where we are going. We are separated from the mystery, the depth, and the greatness of our existence.

We hear the voice of that depth; but our ears are closed. We feel that something radical, total, and unconditioned is demanded of us: but we rebel against it, try to escape its urgency, and will not accept its promise.

We cannot escape, however. If that something is the Ground of our being, we are bound to it for all eternity. Just as we are bound to ourselves and to all other life. We always remain in the power of that from which we are estranged.

That fact brings us to the ultimate depth of sin: separated and yet bound, estranged and yet belonging, destroyed and yet preserved—the state which is called **despair**. Despair means that there is no escape. Despair is "the sickness unto death". But the terrible thing about the sickness of despair is that we cannot be released, not even through open or hidden suicide. For we all know that we are bound eternally and inescapably to the Ground of our being.

The abyss of separation is not always visible. But it has become more visible to our generation than to the preceding generations, because of our feeling of meaninglessness, emptiness, doubt, and cynicism—all expressions of despair, of our separation from the roots and meaning of our life.

Sin in its most profound sense, sin as despair, abounds amongst us.

The Experience of Grace

"Where sin abounded, grace did much more abound," says Paul in the same letter in which he describes the unimaginable power of separation and self-destruction within society and the individual soul. He does not say these words because sentimental interests demand a happy ending for everything tragic. He says them because they describe the most overwhelming and determining experience of his life.

In the picture of Jesus as the Christ, which appeared to him at the moment of his greatest separation from other men, from himself, and from God, he found himself accepted in spite of his being rejected. And when he found that he was accepted, he was able to accept himself and to be reconciled to others. The moment in which grace struck him and overwhelmed him, he was reunited with that to which he belonged, and from which he was estranged in utter strangeness.

Do we know what it means to be struck by grace?.

- It does not mean that we suddenly believe that God exists, or that Jesus is the Savior, or that the Bible contains the truth. To believe that something *is*, is almost contrary to the meaning of grace.

- Furthermore, grace does not mean simply that we are making progress in our moral self-control, in our fight against special faults, and in our relationships to men and to society. Moral progress may be a fruit of grace; but it is not grace itself, and it can even prevent us from receiving grace.

For there is too often a graceless acceptance of Christian doctrines and a graceless battle against the structures of evil in our personalities. Such a graceless relation to God may lead us by necessity either to arrogance or to despair. It would be better to refuse God and the Christ and the Bible than to accept them without grace. For if we accept without grace, we do so in the state of separation, and can only succeed in deepening the separation. We cannot transform our lives unless we allow them to be transformed by that stroke of grace.

It happens; or it does not happen. And certainly it does not happen if we try to force it upon ourselves, just as it shall not happen so long as we think, in our self-complacency, that we have no need of it.

Grace strikes us when we are in great pain and restlessness. It strikes us when we walk through the dark valley of an empty and meaningless life. It strikes us when we feel that our separation is deeper than usual, because we have violated another life—a life which we loved, or from which we were estranged. It strikes us when our disgust for our own being, our indifference, our weakness, our hostility, and our lack of direction and composure have become intolerable to us. It strikes us when, year after year, the longed-for perfection of life does not appear, when the old compulsions reign within us as they have for decades, when despair destroys all joy and courage.

Sometimes at that moment a wave of light breaks into our darkness, and it is as though a voice were saying:

"You are accepted. You are accepted, accepted by that which is greater than you, and the name of which you do not know. Do not ask for the name now; perhaps you will find it later. Do not try to do anything now; perhaps later you will do much. Do not seek for anything; do not perform anything; do not intend anything. Simply accept the fact that you are accepted!".

If that happens to us, we experience grace. After such an experience we may not be better than before, and we may not believe more than before. But everything is transformed. In that moment, grace conquers sin, and reconciliation bridges the gulf of estrangement. And nothing is demanded of this experience, no religious or moral or intellectual presupposition, nothing but acceptance.

The Power of Grace

In the light of this grace, we perceive the power of grace in our relation to others and to ourselves.

- We experience the grace of being able to look frankly into the eyes of another, the miraculous grace of reunion of life with life.

- We experience the grace of understanding each other's words. We understand not merely the literal meaning of the words, but also that which lies behind them, even when they are harsh or angry. For even then there is a longing to break through the walls of separation.

- We experience the grace of being able to accept the life of another, even though it be hostile and harmful to us; for, through grace, we know that it belongs to the same Ground to which we belong, and by which we have been accepted.

- We experience the grace which is able to overcome the tragic separation of the sexes, of the generations, of the nations, of the races, and even the utter strangeness between man and nature. Sometimes grace appears in all these separations to reunite us with those to whom we belong. For life belongs to life.

And in the light of this grace, we perceive the power of grace in our relation to ourselves. We experience moments in which we accept ourselves, because we feel that we have been accepted by that which is greater than we.

If only more such moments were given to us! For it is such moments that make us love our life, that make us accept ourselves, not in our goodness and self-complacency, but in our certainty of the eternal meaning of our life.

We cannot force ourselves to accept ourselves. We cannot compel anyone to accept himself. But sometimes it happens that we receive the power to say "yes" to ourselves, that peace enters into us and makes us whole, that self-hate and self-contempt disappear, and that our self is reunited with itself. Then we can say that grace has come upon us.

"Sin" and "grace" are strange words; but they are not strange things. We find them whenever we look into ourselves with searching eyes and longing hearts. They determine our life. They abound within us and in all of life.

May grace more abound within us!.

Chapter 5
Bible-Inspired Quotations and Prayer

In this chapter I focus on prayer and on reading the inspiring words of God in the Holy Bible. I wrote these reflections while I was caring for my wife during five days in the hospital because of heart failure. During that time she went through three procedures in the operating room.

At last, the doctors brought me good news: there were no blocked arteries, only minor valve problems that could be regulated with medicine. Thank God, my prayers were answered. After only five days we were able to bring her home, where I could continue to take care of her.

My hope is that you, my dear readers, will receive strength from this chapter. When you face shocking or difficult times, you can pray and read the inspired Word of God. His Word brings miracles. The moments I share here truly happened in my life, and I believe they can happen in yours too.

Below are some of the scriptures, short prayers, and daily reflections that encouraged me. I share them so that they may encourage you as well.

Psalm 121:7 (KJV)

"The LORD shall preserve thee from all evil: he shall preserve thy soul."

You might not realize it, but God is blocking the devil's plans all the time.

If you sense that God is protecting you, give Him praise.

Amen.

Start your day with these simple yet powerful prayers:

Forgive me, Lord.

Guide me, Lord.

Protect me, Lord.

Bless me, Lord.

Thank You, Lord.

Amen.

July 25, 2025 – Perspective of the Day

I understand that it can be difficult to make the decision to cut people out of your life.

Remember that your mental and emotional well-being is important. Surround yourself with those who support and uplift you. It is okay to let go of toxic relationships that no longer serve you.

Trust in your inner strength and know that you deserve to be surrounded by positivity and love. Embrace the opportunity to create space for new connections that will bring joy and fulfillment to your life. You are strong, and you are deserving of happiness.

Today is Friday, July 25, 2025

He did it again. God woke us up today.

Take just one minute to thank God!

Amen.

Prayer of Humble Service

Jesus, thank You for showing us what humble service looks like. Today and every day, please show me how to follow the example You have set.

Make me aware of the people in my life whom I can serve selflessly. Let my acts of service reflect my deep love for You and for the people You created.

In Your name, **Amen.**

No matter what you encounter, no matter how big the storms in your life, God is bigger and more powerful than your problems.

Amen.

Those we love walk beside us every day— unseen, unheard, but always near.

They do not go away; still loved, still missed, and always dear.

Friday Prayer

Heavenly Father, thank You for the gift of this Friday and the start of a brand-new weekend. We are grateful for Your love that carries us through each day.

As we wrap up the week, fill our hearts with peace, our minds with clarity, and our souls with joy.

Bless the work we have done, guide our steps ahead, and remind us to rest in Your presence.

May You continue to bless us, heal us, and surround us with a hedge of protection.

In Jesus' name, **Amen.**

Psalm 46:1 "God is our refuge and strength, a very present help in trouble."

God bless you all.

Today is Friday, July 25, 2025

I do not know what the future holds for me, but I firmly believe that God has a wonderful plan for my life.

Amen.

Do We See and Hear?

The parables of Jesus often speak of things we do not have much experience with.

Read and reflect on *Matthew 13:10–13* and ask the Lord to open your spiritual eyes and ears.

GOD, I NEED YOU

Dear Lord, no one knows me better than You.

You know my every thought, need, and desire— why I cry, why I laugh, and why I worry.

When I am weak, You are my strength.

When I am sad, You are my comfort.

When storms come, You are my refuge.

When I am lost, You are my guiding light.

If you are going through a test of faith and you love God, do not be ashamed of Him.

Share this prayer with a friend and see what God will do.

Colossians 3:23 (NKJV) "And whatever you do, do it heartily, as to the Lord and not to men."

Worship is not only sitting in church, raising your hands, or singing Christian songs.

Worship is a lifestyle.

It is seeking to honor and obey God in word, in thought, and in deeds.

If you believe this, say **Amen.**

Strong Prayer

Dear God, thank You for always being there for me.

You hug me when I hurt.

You guide me when I am lost.

You are with me when I feel alone.

I need You every day.

If God has been good to you, don't forget to thank Him.

Amen.

Never Stop Praying

Sometimes God answers in ways you would never expect. **Amen.**

- When your heart is full of anxiety—pray.

- When you feel alone and helpless—pray.

- When you don't know what to do—pray.

- When you feel like there is no way out—pray.

Matthew 7:7 (KJV)

"Ask, and it shall be given you; seek, and ye shall find; knock, and it shall be opened unto you."

God says:

"Those who truly have God-fearing hearts, in both big and small matters, will look to Me, pray to Me, entrust everything to Me, and then see how I lead and guide them. The more you experience this, the more you will feel that looking to Me in all things is very practical."

Dear friend, God's grace is enough to carry you through anything.

Prayer will open the door you need. God is listening, and He will lead you into a brighter future.

"God, I love You, and I want more people to be helped."

Today's Prayer

Dear Lord, thank You for waking me up this morning and giving me the breath of life.

I know that I have reached this day not by luck but by Your grace.

Thank You for all the good things You have done for me.

Today, I commit myself to You; please guide my every step.

In this world that often seems grey, help me to live with a positive mindset.

Let me hear Your voice, follow Your will, and may all I do bring glory to You.

May Your hand lead me through this day.

I pray this in the name of Jesus.

Amen.

Today's Prayer

Lord Jesus,

You came not to be served but to serve, teaching us that true greatness lies in humility and love.

Help us to let go of pride and selfish ambition.

Give us hearts willing to serve, even when it costs, and hands ready to lift others up in love.

Teach us to drink from Your cup with courage, to walk the path of sacrifice with grace, and to find joy in becoming last, that we may be first in Your kingdom.

Amen.

Today is Thursday, July 24, 2025

God says:

"I will always comfort all those who perceive My intentions, and I will not allow them to suffer or come to harm.

The crucial thing now is to take action according to My intentions.

Those who do this will certainly receive My blessings and come under My protection."

If you are reading this, may God remove your pain, worries, and problems and replace them with happiness and peace.

Amen.

Pray This Psalm Before You Go to Bed

Father, as this day comes to an end, I thank You for the rest You have promised.

Hebrews 4:9–10 reminds me that true rest is found in You.

Tonight, I lay down my worries and trust Your peace.

I release the weight of today into Your loving hands.

I surrender my worries, my fears, and my uncertainties about tomorrow.

I trust in Your protection, knowing that You watch over me as I rest.

Guard my dreams, Lord, and fill them with Your peace.

May my sleep be a time of rest for my body, soul, and spirit, knowing that You hold my future securely.

In Jesus' name I pray for peaceful and restorative sleep, trusting in Your care for what lies ahead.

If God is worthy of your praise, say **Amen!**

Our lives go on without you, but nothing is the same.

We hide our heartache when someone speaks your name.

Sad are the hearts that love you, silent are the tears that fall.

Living here without you is the hardest part of all.

You did so many things for us; your heart was kind and true.

When we needed someone, we could always count on you.

The special years will not return when we were all together,

but with the love within our hearts, you walk with us forever.

They do not know how hard it is for me to hold my tears inside.

I lost someone special, and it is very hard for me every day.

I may look strong, and I may have you fooled,

but what you do not realize is that I fight each day to be this way.

Please be patient with me. I will never be the same person I once was.

Just know that I am trying to be the best self I can be today.

Prayer for Today

Dear God, sometimes I want to give up when I face the challenges of life.

But when I remember how much You love me, I am strengthened to face any test, because I know You are with me.

Thank You, God.

Amen.

Today's Prayer – July 25

Dear Father in heaven, Creator of what is good, beautiful, and full of joy, so that all may work in harmony with You,

we thank You for all the good that comes to us. May we be Your children, joined together to serve You.

May our lives bring joy to others, and may we do good without ceasing through Your great, strong love, which moves us, strengthens us, and helps us every day, however hard life may be.

May Your name be praised throughout the world. May Your kingdom come and Your will be done on earth as it is in heaven.

Amen.

Daily Verse

"O LORD, be gracious to us; we wait for thee. Be our arm every morning, our salvation in the time of trouble." — *Isaiah 33:2*

Short Prayer for a Miracle

May God bless you.

Father, I come before You with a humble heart, seeking Your divine intervention in my life.

I believe in Your power to perform miracles and in the boundless love You have for Your children.

I surrender my doubts and fears to You, knowing that nothing is impossible for You.

Grant me the faith to trust in Your perfect timing and the strength to persevere through challenges.

May Your miraculous touch bring healing, restoration, and breakthrough in my situation.

I submit myself to Your will, knowing that You work all things together for my good.

Amen.

Romans 6:23 (KJV) "For the wages of sin is death; but the gift of God is eternal life through Jesus Christ our Lord."

God Says

"I am in the heavens, and I am among all things.

I am keeping watch; I am waiting; I am at your side."

At my lowest, God is my hope.

At my darkest, God is my light.

At my weakest, God is my strength.

At my saddest, God is my comforter.

If God is with you, say **Amen!**

Morning Prayer – July 25, 2025

Heavenly Father, I come before You today asking for forgiveness of my sins.

Lord, thank You for giving me another day to live.

My only request this morning is that You bless my family and friends.

Strengthen their faith.

Let them live with contentment and rejoice in gladness.

Protect them spiritually, physically, mentally, and emotionally.

This I pray in Jesus' name, **Amen.**

The Lord's Prayer *Matthew 6:9–13*

Our Father who art in heaven, hallowed be Thy name.

Thy kingdom come.

Thy will be done on earth, as it is in heaven.

Give us this day our daily bread, and forgive us our trespasses, as we forgive those who trespass against us.

And lead us not into temptation, but deliver us from evil.

For Thine is the kingdom, and the power, and the glory, for ever and ever.

Amen.

Night Prayer

Dear God, before I go to sleep tonight, I want to thank You for everything You have done.

I surrender all my questions and worries to You.

I believe You will continue to make a way for me, just as You have done before.

I may feel tired, discouraged, and anxious, but I will not give up on my faith.

I pray that when I wake up tomorrow, You will inspire me, encourage me, and prepare me for another beautiful day.

I love You.

If God has been good to you, say **Amen.**

Psalm 121:7 (KJV) "The LORD shall preserve thee from all evil: he shall preserve thy soul."

You may not realize it, but God is blocking the devil's plans all the time.

If you feel that God is protecting you, give Him praise.

Amen.

Verse of the Day

"If we confess our sins, he is faithful and just to forgive us our sins, and to cleanse us from all unrighteousness."
— 1 John 1:9 (KJV)

Amen.

Morning Prayer – July 25, 2025

Heavenly Father, I come before You today asking for forgiveness of my sins.

Lord, thank You for giving me another day to live.

My only request this morning is that You bless my family and friends.

Strengthen their faith.

Let them live with contentment and rejoice in gladness.

Protect them spiritually, physically,mentally, and emotionally.

This I pray in Jesus' name, **Amen.**

Saint of the Day – July 25

Saint James the Greater, Pray for Us

Saint James the Greater (died 44 AD) was the brother of Saint John the Apostle and one of Jesus' original twelve apostles.

The title "Greater" was added to distinguish him from Saint James the Lesser.

It is believed to refer not to status or holiness but possibly to his height or age.

James was the son of Zebedee.

He and his brother John left their father and their nets to follow after Jesus.

James was one of the three apostles invited to witness the miraculous Transfiguration of Christ on Mount Tabor.

After Christ's Resurrection and Ascension, James preached the gospel across the Roman Empire and later traveled to Spain, where he spread the gospel for many years.

The famous *Camino de Santiago* pilgrimage in Spain is named in his honor ("Santiago" is Spanish for James).

At the end of his life, James returned to Jerusalem, where he became the first apostle to be martyred.

His feast day is July 25.

Jeremiah 33:3 (NIV) "Call to me and I will answer you and tell you great and unsearchable things you do not know."

Amen.

Good morning.

Prayer for Today – July 25, 2025

Heavenly Father, thank You for today's new mercies.

Help me stay focused on Your Word and walk in the freedom You have given me.

I declare that no weapon formed against me shall prosper, and I stand firm in Your protection.

Let Your Holy Spirit guide my every move and help me to be a vessel of Your love.

I pray for peace in my heart and clarity in my mind, so that I can face whatever comes my way.

May Your wisdom lead me to breakthrough moments.

In Jesus' name, **Amen.**

Dear God, before I go to sleep tonight, I do not have any specific requests.

I simply want to express my gratitude for everything You have done for me.

Lord, I place all my problems and worries in Your hands, trusting that You will resolve them for me.

There are times when I feel tired, discouraged, and anxious, but I will not leave You.

I hope that tomorrow You will continue to inspire me and walk beside me.

I love You.

Morning Prayer – July 25, 2025

Dear ever-loving and caring Lord, thank You for the love You have poured upon me and my family.

As I begin this day, Lord, everywhere I walk, let it be on Your path.

Everything I see, let me see through Your eyes.

Everything I do, let it be according to Your will.

For every hardship I face, let me place it in Your hands.

Every emotion I feel, let it be Your Spirit moving in me.

Everything I seek, let me find it in Your love.

My dear God, I thank You for this day.

I ask not to know where I am going, but only to know and feel deep in my heart and soul that You are with me, that You are guiding me, that I am safe in the protection of Your loving care.

In Jesus' name, I offer myself to You.

Amen.

Grace is when God gives us good things we do not deserve.

Mercy is when He spares us from bad things we do deserve.

Blessings are when He is generous with both.

Truly, we can never run out of reasons to thank Him.

God is good all the time!

Pray Before You Go to Bed

Dear Heavenly Father, as I prepare to sleep, I come before You asking for peaceful rest.

Psalm 4:8 (KJV) "I will both lay me down in peace, and sleep: for thou, LORD, only makest me dwell in safety."

Lord, I surrender today's burdens into Your hands, laying down all my worries, fears, and anxieties.

Please watch over me as I rest and cover me with Your peace.

May my body and soul find true rest under Your protection, for I know You are always watching over me and safeguarding my future.

I pray this in Jesus' name.

If God is good to you, praise Him!

Amen.

Tonight's Prayer

Dear God, before I go to sleep tonight, I don't have any specific requests.

I simply want to express my gratitude for everything You have done for me.

Lord, I place all my problems and worries in Your hands, trusting that You will resolve them for me.

There are times when I feel tired, discouraged, and anxious, but I will not leave You.

I hope that tomorrow You will continue to inspire me and walk alongside me.

I love You.

God, I Need You

Every day, every moment, every second, as long as I am breathing, I need You.

I cannot face this world alone.

O God, You are the only reason I have made it this far!

I pray that You will never let go of my hand in the year 2025.

If you feel that God has been protecting you since your birth, take a moment to thank Him.

Amen.

Nighttime Prayer

Dear God, before I go to sleep tonight, I don't have any specific requests.

I simply want to express my gratitude for everything You have done for me.

Lord, I place all my problems and worries in Your hands, trusting that You will resolve them for me.

There are times when I feel tired, discouraged, and anxious, but I will not leave You.

I hope that tomorrow You will continue to inspire me and walk alongside me.

I love You.

Amen.

"I Never Left You" John F. Connor

I never left you.

I watch you every day.

I am always very near.

I know deep in your heart you realize I am here.

I watch you while you sleep in your bed at home.

I hear you when you speak to me when you are on your own.

You cannot understand the reason why I have gone,

but I will never leave you; I am there to keep you strong.

Talk to me—I hear you, though you may not see.

We share an unbroken bond that will always be.

Death won't keep us apart, for our love is forever.

Just remember me in your heart, and one day we will be together.

Live your life and live it full; don't waste a single day.

Remember I am always with you, every step of the way.

Psalm 139:7–10 (NKJV) "Where can I go from Your Spirit? Or where can I flee from Your presence? If I ascend into heaven, You are there; If I make my bed in hell, behold, You are there.

If I take the wings of the morning, And dwell in the uttermost parts of the sea, Even there Your hand shall lead me, And Your right hand shall hold me."

Good Morning

O Lord, our good and gracious God, I come before You with a heart full of gratitude.

You have been with me every step of the way, and I am thankful for Your presence.

As I look forward to the weekend, help me maintain a heart of thanksgiving and a spirit of contentment and joy.

Teach me to love You and everyone around me, now and always.

Amen.

Morning Prayer – July 23, 2025

Heavenly Father, every morning I wake up, I am blessed.

Your words in Psalm 118:24 assure me:

"This is the day the LORD has made; let us rejoice and be glad in it."

Today, I place my plans and expectations in Your loving hands.

No matter how much drama is in my life or how much pain my body may be in, I know in my heart that You are watching over me.

May my day be a time of blessing, a renewal of body, soul, and spirit, knowing that You are in control of my life.

In Jesus' name I pray.

If God has always been with you, say **Amen.**

Morning Prayer – July 25, 2025

Heavenly Father, I come before You today asking for forgiveness of my sins.

Lord, thank You for giving me another day to live.

My only request this morning is that You bless my family and friends.

Strengthen their faith.

Let them live with contentment and rejoice in gladness.

Protect them spiritually, physically, mentally, and emotionally.

This I pray in Jesus' name, **Amen.**

Tonight's Prayer – July 24, 2025

Dear God,

Before I go to sleep tonight, I want to thank You for everything.

I trust You with all my problems and worries, knowing that You will make a way, just as You have done before.

Even though I feel tired, discouraged, and frustrated, I won't lose faith.

Please refresh me as I sleep, renew my spirit, and prepare me for tomorrow.

I am counting on You to give me the strength I need to face whatever comes my way.

I love You.

In Jesus' name, **Amen.**

Verse of the Day – April 30, 2025

"His divine power has granted to us all things that pertain to life and godliness, through the knowledge of him who called us to his own glory and excellence." — 1 Peter 1:3

In Jesus' Name, Do Not Ignore This Prayer

Dear Heavenly Father, I come before You today seeking Your protection from all forms of evil. Surround me with Your divine light and guard me from both visible and invisible harm. Strengthen me to resist temptation and guide me away from every path that leads to darkness.

Fill me with Your Holy Spirit. Help me to stand firm in my faith and resist every influence of evil. I ask for Your protection over my loved ones, my home, and my community. May Your peace and love overcome all dark forces.

Lord, I promise to share this prayer, so that You may use it to bless someone else through me.

In Jesus Christ's name I pray, **Amen.**

Put "Amen" and disappoint Satan!

Saturday Prayer

(Written by Fr. Ronald Rey P. Espartinez, SVD)

Almighty Father, I praise and thank You for the gift of life and this new day. I adore and worship You as Lord, Creator, and Healer of my life.

Help me to be always attentive to Your divine presence in my life, in my family, and even in my worst moments. Remind me that You are my Father, my consoler, my refuge, and the reason for my existence.

Forgive me of my sins and guide me so that I may face and correct the weaknesses in my character and behavior. Direct my heart always in the way of light, hope, and peace.

Bless my family, friends, and relatives with good health, healing of emotions, material provision, and harmony in their relationships.

In Jesus' name, **Amen.**

God Wants You to Pray for Tomorrow with Hope

Dear Heavenly Father, thank You for being with me today. Thank You for Your peace and protection, for guiding me through every challenge, and for lifting me when I felt weary.

Lord, I invite You into my tomorrow. Please go before me and lead every path. Give me clear eyes to see opportunities, a tender heart to care for others, and strong faith to move forward with courage. Let me not live for myself alone, but make me a vessel of blessing.

"For I know the plans I have for you," declares the LORD, "plans to prosper you and not to harm you, plans to give you a future and a hope." — Jeremiah 29:11

Lord, I place my loved ones into Your hands. Keep them safe, healthy, and joyful. Whatever we face tomorrow, may Your presence never leave us.

If I feel weak tomorrow, remind me that Your power is made perfect in weakness. If I find success, remind me that it is all by Your grace and mercy.

I believe with all my heart that because You are with me, tomorrow will bring new grace, new opportunities, and new hope. Lord, use me to share this prayer so that more people may look to You with faith for tomorrow.

In Jesus' name I pray, **Amen.**

If you believe God holds tomorrow, write: **"God is Good."**

Pray for One Minute and the Enemy Will Not Come Near You

Almighty God, my Father, I come before You in the victorious name of Jesus Christ.

At this moment, I declare that the enemy has no right to touch my mind, my emotions, my body, or my future. Your true light shines into every dark corner of my life—lies, fear, and confusion must flee!

Lord, You are my shield and my firm foundation; I will not be shaken. In the name of Jesus, I rebuke every hidden force of darkness. Whether it disguises itself as heaviness, anxiety, or exhaustion, it must leave completely now.

I choose not to be ruled by atmosphere or emotions; I choose to stand on Your Word and walk in Your light.

Lord, send Your angels to surround and protect me. Make my heart strong and my faith unwavering. My victory is not based on my feelings but on the finished work You have already done.

I pray this in the glorious and victorious name of Jesus Christ, **Amen.**

Strong Prayer

Dear Lord, I am not perfect. Please forgive my sins.

I love You and I will always need You.

Cover my family, my home, my work, my dreams, my projects, and my friends with Your precious blood. Grant me health and strength.

Lord, I promise to share this prayer so You can work through me.

Put **"Amen"** and let the devil be disappointed.

Today's Prayer – Hope

Dear God, thank You for giving me hope. Even when life is hard, You remind me that I have what I need when I draw near to You.

You are my strength and my peace, in good times and in tough times.

Help me stay close to You today and keep my heart in the right place.

Amen.

Isaiah 40:31 – Strength in Waiting

Isaiah 40:31 (KJV) "But they that wait upon the LORD shall renew their strength; they shall mount up with wings as eagles; they shall run, and not be weary; and they shall walk, and not faint."

When God pushes you to the edge of difficulty… **trust Him fully.**

Two things can happen:

Either He will catch you when you fall, or He will teach you how to fly.

Trust Him forever.

If He has carried you through storms, forward this in your heart and say a true **Amen.**

Today's Prayer (Refrain)

Dear God, thank You for giving me hope.

Even when life is hard, You remind me that I have what I need when I come close to You.

You are my strength and peace, in good times and in tough times.

Help me stay close to You today and keep my heart in the right place.

Amen.

A Prayer of Thanksgiving and Surrender

Dear Lord, I come before You to thank You for the love and grace You have poured upon me.

Thank You for granting me strength to win the battles of everyday life.

Lord, I do not know what I will face today, but I know that You are watching over me at every moment.

I am willing to walk in Your will.

Please continue to guide me to make the right choices.

If you believe, offer an **"Amen"** and share this blessing with those you love.

A Blessing You Didn't Know You Needed

Dear Jesus, thank You for everything You have done for us— for taking on so much so that we could find true freedom and new life through Your resurrection.

Today, we celebrate that You defeated death and brought us life.

Thank You for Your endless grace that frees us from sin and wraps us in Your love.

Please guide us every day to live in a way that shines Your glory and grace.

If you believe this, pass this message to someone who needs it and proclaim a devoted **Amen.**

2 Corinthians 12:9 – Grace in Weakness

2 Corinthians 12:9 (KJV) "And he said unto me, My grace is sufficient for thee: for my strength is made perfect in weakness.

Most gladly therefore will I rather glory in my infirmities, that the power of Christ may rest upon me."

Jacob lied.

Moses murdered.

Saul persecuted Christians.

David committed adultery.

Peter denied Jesus.

God used every single one of these people to build His Kingdom.

You are never too far gone for God to use.

Don't let the devil steal your story— let Christ rewrite it.

If you believe in God, take a minute to thank Him.

A Prayer for Your Family

Dear Heavenly Father, I lift up my family to You today.

I cannot control what life brings their way, but I trust in Your guidance and care.

Please watch over them, keep them safe, and draw them close to You.

Amen.

Morning Prayer – Grace for a New Day

Heavenly Father, thank You for waking me up to a new day.

I trust in Your Word, as it is written:

Numbers 6:24–26 (KJV) "The LORD bless thee, and keep thee: The LORD make his face shine upon thee, and be gracious unto thee: The LORD lift up his countenance upon thee, and give thee peace."

Today, I come before You, laying down my worries, my challenges, and all the uncertainty about the future.

I trust in Your perfect plan and timing for my life.

Even when I do not understand, I know You have already made a way for me.

Lord, fill my heart and mind with Your peace.

Let this day be a blessed one, refreshing my body, soul, and spirit, because I know my life is in Your hands.

In Jesus' name, I ask for wisdom, strength, and joy to move forward in Your grace.

Amen.

Strong Prayer in Times of Worry

Dear Lord, I need Your help.

Lately I have been so worried about things that are out of my control.

Help me to trust that You are working out every little detail of my life.

I don't want to live in fear, and I don't want to doubt You.

I want to fully trust You in all that I go through.

So Lord, please increase my faith and teach me to keep my eyes on You when it is hard to do so.

I need You.

I cannot do this on my own.

In Jesus' name I pray.

If you love God and are not ashamed of Him, let someone you love read this prayer.

If this prayer brings you peace, simply echo **Amen.**

God will carry you through every storm in your life and give you strength to make it.

Our God is so awesome.

Morning Prayer – August 9, 2025

Lord, as a new day begins, I come before You with an open heart.

You know my life—what worries me, how I feel, what I think, what I long for, what I lack, and what I desire.

In moments of darkness, You are my light.

In storms, You are my peace.

In sadness, You are my strength.

In loneliness, You are my companion.

I hold onto Your promise, for Your Word says:

Isaiah 41:10 (KJV) "Fear thou not; for I am with thee: be not dismayed; for I am thy God: I will strengthen thee; yea, I will help thee; yea, I will uphold thee with the right hand of my righteousness."

I surrender this day into Your loving hands, knowing You are always with me.

If God is good to you, praise Him.

Amen.

Today Is Saturday

God says: "Do not worry about how tomorrow will be, nor how the future will be.

As long as you rely on Me to live each day, I will surely lead you."

Heavenly Father, every morning I wake up, I am blessed.

No matter how much drama is in my life or how much pain my body may be in, I know in my heart that You are watching over me.

If our Father is welcome in your home 365 days a year, say **Amen.**

Tonight's Prayer – August 9, 2025

Lord, You have blessed us again today more than we could ask or think.

Thank You for Your loving care, and for the grace and mercy that sustained us throughout the day.

May You surround us with Your protective angels and allow us to rest peacefully tonight until the morning light.

In Jesus' name, **Amen.**

"Whatever you do for your family, for your children, for your husband, for your wife, you do for God. All we do—our prayers, our work, our suffering—is for Jesus." — *Blessed Mother Teresa*

God Wants You to Read This Verse

Isaiah 41:10 (KJV) "Fear thou not; for I am with thee: be not dismayed; for I am thy God: I will strengthen thee; yea, I will help thee; yea, I will uphold thee with the right hand of my righteousness."

Stop stressing yourself out.

God knows you are tired.

He knows you are trying.

Trust Him.

He will make a way where there seems to be no way.

If you have faith that this same God can turn your situation around, and you depend on Him right now, take one minute and say: **"I DO."**

Micah 7:7 – Faith That Waits

Micah 7:7 (KJV) "Therefore I will look unto the LORD; I will wait for the God of my salvation: my God will hear me."

Faith will make you wait.

Faith will make you persevere.

Faith will make you see the promise.

If you have faith in God, can I get your **"Amen"**?

Morning Prayer – August 11, 2025

Dear God, thank You for waking me up to another beautiful day.

I am grateful for Your protection and provision.

Please fill me with peace, strength, and wisdom as I face today's challenges.

May I live in a way that honors You.

In Jesus' name, **Amen.**

Monday Prayer

(Written by Fr. Ronald Rey P. Espartinez, SVD)

Almighty Father, thank You for my life.

Thank You for the many times You came to my rescue and embraced and lifted me in the past.

Father, I believe I have come this far in my journey and reached this level of understanding and growth because of Your unending love, trust, patience, and faithfulness in my life.

Today, I ask You to light and guide my thoughts, feelings, dreams, and behavior.

Help me not to give in to excessive fear or worry.

Bless me with a positive mindset, a hopeful heart, and a persevering spirit so that I may keep going forward in my journey.

I surrender everything to You this new week— my plans, my family, my health, and my future.

In Jesus' name, **Amen.**

Morning Prayer – August 11, 2025

Dear God, as morning comes, I thank You for the gift of life.

Please give me strength and wisdom for today.

Bless this day with healing, blessing, and miracles.

Keep my family and friends safe.

Thank You for this new day.

Please stay with us.

In Jesus' name, **Amen.**

Night Prayer

Dear God, before I go to sleep tonight, I just want to thank You for everything You have done.

I surrender all my questions and worries to You.

I believe that You will continue to make a way for me, just as You have before.

I may be tired, discouraged, and anxious, but I will not give up on my faith.

I pray that when I wake up tomorrow, You will inspire me, encourage me, and prepare me for another beautiful day.

I love You.

If God has been good to you, say **Amen.**

Tuesday Prayer

(Written by Fr. Ronald Rey P. Espartinez, SVD)

Almighty Father, thank You for the gift of life.

Thank You for giving me another opportunity to come closer to You and to feel Your love for me.

Under Your fatherly care, waking up in the morning is a beautiful occasion, because I know there is a loving and faithful God who is ready to welcome, believe, accept, and nourish me each day.

Thank You for being my Father and the Lord of my life, because You constantly fill my life with Your light, meaning, guidance, and healing grace.

I entrust to You my health, my family, my problems, and my plans today.

Please forgive me of my sins; lead me on Your path, help me correct my mistakes, and grant me courage to face my trials and pains.

In Jesus' name, **Amen.**

Morning Prayer – August 12, 2025

Dear God, thank You so much for the gift of life and for allowing me to see another blessed day.

Let this day be a day of miracles.

May Your holy angels protect my family not only today but every day.

Please keep my friends safe in Your care.

Lord, before I start this day, I surrender all my plans to You and ask that Your will be done in my life.

This I pray in the precious name of Jesus, **Amen.**

Tonight's Prayer – August 11, 2025

Dear God, thank You so much for all the blessings You have given me throughout the day.

Thank You for keeping my family safe and for giving us good health.

As we prepare for bed tonight, we ask for Your divine protection and a peaceful night of sleep.

We commit our plans and our lives to You.

We have many problems right now, but we choose to surrender everything to You.

Amen.

Morning Prayer – Daily Surrender

Dear Lord, thank You for waking me up this morning and giving me the breath of life.

I know that I have reached this day not by luck but by Your grace.

Thank You for all the good things You have done for me.

Today, I commit myself to You; please guide my every step.

In this world that often seems grey, help me to live with a positive mindset.

Let me hear Your voice, follow Your will, and may all I do bring glory to You.

May Your hand lead me through this day.

I pray in the name of Jesus.

If God is good to you, praise Him.

Amen.

Joel 2:25–26 – God Restores

Joel 2:25–26 (paraphrased) God will restore to you what you have lost.

Hold on—His plans are always worth the wait.

Five Promises from God to Start Your Day with Faith

1. God is with me.

2. God has a beautiful plan for me.

3. God will guide my path.

4. God will protect my peace.

5. God will carry my burdens.

Woman of God, even if you are busy, if you love Him, offer your **Amen.**

Start Your Morning with This Simple but Powerful Prayer

Dear Lord, thank You for the gift of another day.

Thank You for waking me up, for breath in my lungs, and hope in my heart.

I know I do not walk through today alone— Your grace goes before me and Your love surrounds me.

You have carried me through so much, and I trust You to carry me through this day too.

Help me to see people the way You do, to respond with kindness, and to walk in peace no matter what comes.

Guide my steps, guard my heart, and use my life to reflect Your goodness.

In Jesus' name, **Amen.**

If you are starting your day with faith, say **"Amen"** in your heart and let this prayer bless someone else.

Morning Prayer – August 16, 2025

Lord, as a new day begins, I come before You with an open heart.

You know my life—what worries me, how I feel, what I think, what I long for, what I lack, and what I desire.

In moments of darkness, You are my light.

In storms, You are my peace.

In sadness, You are my strength.

In loneliness, You are my companion.

I hold onto Your promise:

Isaiah 41:10 (KJV) "Fear thou not; for I am with thee: be not dismayed; for I am thy God: I will strengthen thee; yea, I will help thee; yea, I will uphold thee with the right hand of my righteousness."

I surrender this day into Your loving hands, knowing You are always with me.

If God is good to you, praise Him.

Amen.

Evening Prayer – August 16, 2025

Heavenly Father, as the day fades into night, we thank You for Your guidance and blessings.

Forgive our missteps, grant us peace, and renew our strength.

Watch over us and our loved ones, shielding us with Your love.

May we rest in Your grace, prepared for tomorrow.

Amen.

Saturday Prayer

(Written by Fr. Ronald Rey P. Espartinez, SVD)

Almighty Father, thank You for my life.

Thank You for being my light and my salvation.

Your light in my heart helps me see that there is always hope and purpose in my life.

Continue to dwell in me—in my mind, heart, and soul.

Cover my whole being with Your divine mercy and power.

Bless me today with a patient heart, a persevering spirit, and a positive mindset, so that I may be driven to move forward and achieve my goals despite trials and setbacks.

Father, I acknowledge You as the foundation of my being.

Trials may shake me for a while, but I will never be uprooted, because You are my refuge, my peace, and my strength.

In Jesus' name, **Amen.**

God Wants You to Read This Today

Psalm 46:10 (KJV) "Be still, and know that I am God."

God allowed Peter to sink in the water, but He never let him drown.

God allowed Daniel to be thrown into the lions' den, but He shut the mouths of the lions.

God allowed Shadrach, Meshach, and Abednego to step into the fire, but He walked with them in the flames.

God does not promise a life without trials, but He does promise to be with you through them.

What feels like a setback is often a setup for something greater.

Trust Him, even in the struggle.

He is always in control.

If you are trusting God for something greater, say **"Amen"** in your heart and share hope with someone today.

Morning Prayer – August 17, 2025

Heavenly Father, I come before You today asking for forgiveness of my sins.

Lord, thank You for giving me another day to live.

My only request this morning is that You bless my family and friends.

Strengthen their faith.

Let them live with contentment and rejoice in gladness.

Protect them spiritually, physically, mentally, and emotionally.

This I pray in Jesus' name, **Amen.**

Tonight's Prayer

Heavenly Father, thank You for Your protection all day long.

Thank You for giving us strength to overcome life's struggles.

You are the reason we remain strong and firm.

Tonight, please be with each of us as we rest.

Keep us from harm and danger, and let us wake up tomorrow with refreshed minds.

Thank You for always hearing our prayers.

This I pray in Jesus' name, **Amen.**

Exodus 14:14 – The Lord Fights for You

Exodus 14:14 (KJV) "The LORD shall fight for you, and ye shall hold your peace."

There will always be trials and tribulations in life, but God will carry you through every storm and give you strength to overcome.

If God has been good to you, praise Him and say **Amen.**

Sunday Prayer

(Written by Fr. Ronald Rey P. Espartinez, SVD)

All-powerful Father, thank You for the gift of this new day.

Thank You for giving me another chance to be filled with Your forgiveness, light, strength, and compassion.

Your presence in my life brightens my whole being—mind, heart, and soul.

You motivate me to keep going on in my journey.

With You at my side, my life finds meaning and purpose despite struggles and pain.

Help me to constantly put my faith and hope in Your grace and love for me.

Help me live the life You have entrusted to me with deep reason and direction.

Please forgive my past sins.

Bless my family and friends and keep us always in Your loving embrace.

In Jesus' name, **Amen.**

Night Prayer

Heavenly Father, as I lay down to sleep, I release the weight of the day into Your hands.

Thank You for guiding me through every moment, even the ones I did not understand.

Calm my thoughts, quiet my heart, and wrap me in Your peace.

Protect my loved ones and cover this night with Your presence.

I trust You with tomorrow, for You are already there.

In Jesus' name, **Amen.**

God has already gone before you, preparing beautiful things you cannot yet imagine.

Your prayers are not forgotten.

Heaven is not silent.

God moves with purpose, not pressure.

Your timeline is not delayed— it is divinely timed.

It is easy to feel discouraged when others seem to move ahead while you are still waiting.

But your journey is not meant to look like theirs.

Your story is sacred, unique, and unfolding exactly as it should.

God is not in a rush with you—He is intentional.

Every season, even the quiet ones, is being used to shape you into someone who can carry the very blessings you have been praying for.

God Wants You to Read This Verse Again

Isaiah 41:10 (KJV) "Fear thou not; for I am with thee: be not dismayed; for I am thy God: I will strengthen thee; yea, I will help thee; yea, I will uphold thee with the right hand of my righteousness."

Stop stressing yourself.

God knows you are tired.

He knows you are trying.

Trust Him.

He will make a way where there seems to be no way.

If you believe that this same God can turn your situation around, and if you depend on Him right now, take a minute and say: **"I DO."**

Micah 7:7 – Faith That Perseveres

Micah 7:7 (KJV) "Therefore I will look unto the LORD; I will wait for the God of my salvation: my God will hear me."

Faith will make you wait.

Faith will make you persevere.

Faith will make you see the promise.

If you have faith in God, can I get your **Amen**?

Morning Prayer – August 18, 2025

Dear Lord, thank You for another beautiful sunrise.

Thank You for the gift of life.

Every breath I take is a gift from You.

Thank You for being my constant.

As I begin today, I pray for Your presence to be with us always.

Thank You in advance for the strength that will sustain me, the wisdom that will guide me, and the peace that will fill me.

In Jesus' name I pray, **Amen.**

Seven Promises of God You Can Stand On

1. He will never abandon you.

2. His love for you will never fail.

3. He listens when you pray.

4. He gives peace that the world cannot give.

5. His Word is always true.

6. He will guide your steps.

7. He will turn trials into victories.

Whatever season you are in, remember: God is faithful.

Trust Him, keep believing, and watch Him work in your life.

Say **Amen** if you believe this, and let it bless someone today.

August 18, 2025 – A Word from God

God is saying to you today:

"I have heard your prayers and seen your tears, and I am moving on your behalf.

Just as I added years to the life of Hezekiah, I am adding life, strength, and opportunities to you.

I am bringing healing to your body, your mind, and your circumstances.

The report of man will not override My word over you.

Expect a turnaround that will surprise those around you.

You are not at the end; you are stepping into a renewed chapter.

My answer is **yes**."

Today Is Monday

God says: "Do not worry about how tomorrow will be, nor how the future will be.

As long as you rely on Me to live each day, I will surely lead you."

Heavenly Father, every morning I wake up, I am blessed.

No matter how much drama is in my life or how much pain my body may be in, I know in my heart that You are watching over me.

If you believe in God and are not ashamed of Him, let your heart say **Amen.**

August 18, 2025

He did it again. He woke us up today.

It only takes one minute to thank God.

Amen!

Morning Prayer

August 19, 2025

Lord, thank You for this morning.

Thank You for the life You have lent to me.

Every day You protect me, and I am grateful for all Your love and every blessing You have given me.

Lord, I ask forgiveness for all my sins, my shortcomings, and my mistakes.

Thank You that You are always by my side.

I place all my problems and worries into Your hands.

Lord, please guide me at all times as I live my life here on earth.

Amen.

August 19, 2025

God is saying to you today:

"You must learn to trust My timing.

You can be sure that right now I am arranging all the pieces to come together and work out My plan for your life.

I have been working in your favor long before you encountered this problem.

Don't grow impatient and try to force doors open.

Don't try to make things happen in your own strength.

The answer will come— and it will be right on time."

Morning Prayer

Today is August 19, 2025

Lord, as a new day begins, I come before You with an open heart.

You know my life—what worries me, how I feel, what I think, what I long for, what I lack, and what I desire.

In moments of darkness, You are my light.

In storms, You are my peace.

In sadness, You are my strength.

In loneliness, You are my companion.

I hold onto Your promise, for Your Word says:

Isaiah 41:10 (KJV) "Fear thou not; for I am with thee: be not dismayed; for I am thy God: I will strengthen thee; yea, I will help thee; yea, I will uphold thee with the right hand of my righteousness."

I surrender this day into Your loving hands, knowing You are always with me.

If God is good to you, praise Him.

Amen.

Tuesday Prayer

Dear God, thank You for waking me up to see a new day.

Please give me the energy and strength I need to accomplish all that lies ahead.

Help me keep my eyes fixed on You and not on the worries of the world.

Help me not to be anxious, worried, or stressed.

I commit this day and everything in it into Your hands and ask for Your love, joy, and peace to fill my heart.

In Jesus' name I pray, **Amen.**

Dear God, I humbly ask for strength and wisdom to always stand firm in the face of adversity and to uphold the values that reflect Your teachings.

May I be a beacon of kindness and compassion, spreading Your light to those around me.

Grant me patience to understand others, empathy to embrace their differences, and courage to do what is right.

Help me, Lord, to be an instrument of Your peace.

Let Your love and grace guide my actions.

Amen.

God Wants You to Read This Verse

See Exodus 14:14

Everything is going to be alright.

God knows you are tired and that you have done your best.

He understands your worries about the future.

Do not be afraid— He is always watching over you and sees your perseverance and your refusal to give up.

God is making a way for you right now.

Don't give up. You are going to make it, no matter what it looks like at this moment.

Remember: God is working behind the scenes for your good.

He did not bring you this far to leave you.

Be ready— something you prayed for is about to happen.

Have faith and you will not have to fight in your own strength.

God will move the wrong people out of the way.

He will open the door you could not open and turn the situation around.

If you trust Him, say **Amen** in your heart.

A Reflection on Working with the Heart

If we hire someone only with money, we will receive only their labor.

But if we want them to work with joy and stay with us for a long time, we must also work with heart.

No matter how powerful or important we become, we must remember to consider the hearts of others.

In the end, a good leader is not the one who sits "above" their people, but the one who lives in their hearts.

Never Start Your Day Without This Prayer

Dear God, I thank You for giving me a new day to begin.

I pray that You watch over me, my family, and everyone in need of Your grace.

Protect us, guide us, and fill our hearts with Your peace.

Forgive me for my weaknesses, and strengthen my faith in You.

Where God is, nothing is missing.

Lord, I place everything in Your hands.

Your plan is always perfect, and Your love never fails.

Where there is faith, there is love.

Where there is love, there is peace.

Where there is peace, there is God.

If you depend on God, say in your heart: **"I do."**

"For with God nothing shall be impossible."

Never forget: nothing is more powerful than prayer, nothing is stronger than faith, and nothing is greater than God.

Amen.

August 19, 2025 – Day 231 of 365

God is saying to you today:

"I will provide exactly what you need at just the right time.

My Word in Genesis 22:14 says:

'So Abraham called that place The LORD Will Provide.

And to this day it is said, "On the mountain of the LORD it will be provided."'

You may not see how it will all come together, but I already have a way.

Keep trusting— I am your Provider."

Morning Prayer

August 20, 2025

Good morning, Lord.

It is another day, and I thank You for letting me experience another miracle of life.

Despite the challenges, You never fail to bless us and to take care of us.

As this day begins, may You cover me and my family with Your blood and keep us safe for the rest of the day.

In Jesus' name, **Amen.**

Morning Prayer – Wednesday, August 20

Lord God of heaven and earth, thank You for the gift of this new day.

As the sun rises, may Your light shine upon our thoughts, our words, and our actions.

Strengthen our hearts to walk in humility, love, and mercy, that we may serve You and others with joy.

Help us to turn away from distractions and focus on the beauty of Your will.

Grant peace to our minds, healing to those in pain, and hope to those who feel lost.

Guide our steps, O Lord, that everything we do today may glorify Your holy name.

In Jesus' name we pray, **Amen.**

"The steadfast love of the LORD never ceases; his mercies never come to an end; they are new every morning; great is your faithfulness." — Lamentations 3:22–23

Mid-Day Prayer

Wednesday, August 20

Lord Jesus, as we pause in the middle of this day, we lift up our hearts to You.

Grant us strength to continue our work with patience,

wisdom to make the right choices, and peace in the midst of all challenges.

Fill us with Your grace, O Lord, so that every word and action reflects Your love.

Stay with us, guide us, and bless the rest of this day.

Amen.

Today Is Wednesday – August 20, 2025

God says:

"Do not worry about how tomorrow will be, nor how the future will be.

As long as you rely on Me to live each day, I will surely lead you."

It is a beautiful thing to wake up in the morning knowing that God has given you another day to live.

Take one minute to thank God.

Amen.

Five Prayers for Wednesday

August 20, 2025

1. **Lord,** remove any laziness or procrastination from my mind and body.

2. Push me to my full potential.

3. **Dear God,** please bring peace to my confusion, joy to my sadness, and hope to my heart.

4. **Dear God,** if something is not for me, remove it.

5. If certain people are not meant for me, reveal it.

6. End anything in my life that is not part of Your plan.

7. **Lord,** protect the path I am on and do not let me quit for anything.

8. **Dear God,** please calm my mind, heal my heart, and take my worries away.

Amen.

August 21, 2025

In another language it is said:

No one knows how long we will remain here on earth.

So stay calm, be humble, do good to others, and always pray to our God.

Amen.

Morning Prayer

August 21, 2025

Lord, thank You for this new morning.

Thank You for the gift of life and Your continual love for me and my family.

I pray for Your protection and guidance.

Please bless this day ahead.

In Jesus' name, **Amen.**

Today Is Thursday

God says:

"Do not worry about how tomorrow will be, nor how the future will be.

As long as you rely on Me to live each day, I will surely lead you."

Heavenly Father, every morning I wake up, I am blessed.

No matter how much drama is in my life or how much pain my body feels, I know in my heart that You are watching over me.

If you believe in God and are not ashamed of Him, say **Amen.**

Morning Prayer

Today is August 21, 2025

Lord, as a new day begins, I come before You with an open heart.

You know my life—what worries me, how I feel, what I think, what I long for, what I lack, and what I desire.

In moments of darkness, You are my light.

In storms, You are my peace.

In sadness, You are my strength.

In loneliness, You are my companion.

I hold onto Your promise, for Your Word says:

Isaiah 41:10 (KJV) "Fear thou not; for I am with thee: be not dismayed; for I am thy God: I will strengthen thee; yea, I will help thee; yea, I will uphold thee with the right hand of my righteousness."

I surrender this day into Your loving hands, knowing You are always with me.

If God is good to you, praise Him.

Amen.

Morning Prayer

August 22, 2025

Lord, thank You for the gift of life, allowing me and my family to see another beautiful day.

Today, Lord, we open our home to You.

May You bring healing, blessings, and miracles as You come into our lives.

In Jesus' name, **Amen.**

Thankful Thursday

Heavenly Father, on this Thankful Thursday, we come before You with hearts full of gratitude.

You are our Provider, our Protector, and our ever-present help in times of need.

Thank You for the breath in our lungs and the countless blessings, seen and unseen, that You pour into our lives.

In every season, You are faithful.

When we are weak, You strengthen us.

When we are afraid, You remind us that You are our refuge.

Thank You for guiding our steps, for opening doors we never expected, and for closing the ones that were never meant for us.

Fill our hearts with peace today, Lord.

Let us shine Your light and share Your love with those around us.

We praise You, we honor You, and we give You all the glory.

In Jesus' name, **Amen.**

Morning Prayer

Today is August 22, 2025

Lord, as a new day begins, I come before You with an open heart.

You know my life—what worries me, how I feel, what I think, what I long for, what I lack, and what I desire.

In moments of darkness, You are my light.

In storms, You are my peace.

In sadness, You are my strength.

In loneliness, You are my companion.

I hold onto Your promise, for Your Word says:

Isaiah 41:10 (KJV) "Fear thou not; for I am with thee: be not dismayed; for I am thy God: I will strengthen thee; yea, I will help thee; yea, I will uphold thee with the right hand of my righteousness."

I surrender this day into Your loving hands, knowing You are always with me.

If God is good to you, praise Him.

Amen.

Quiet Reflection

Take time to sit alone in silence.

Think about what you have done and what has happened each day.

Consider the mistakes that need to be corrected tomorrow.

Ask yourself:

- Did I do anything that was not right?
- Did I do anything that hurt or displeased someone?

Bring these things before God, and let Him correct and guide your heart.

Thank You, God, for carrying me through all the hard times and for never letting me go.

Amen.

Friday Morning Prayer

Heavenly Father, as the sun rises on this Friday, I pause in Your presence with a heart full of gratitude.

Thank You for walking with me through the joys and trials of this week.

Your faithfulness has been my anchor, Your love my refuge.

Lord, as I step into this day, help me to carry Your peace into every moment.

Let my words be gentle, my actions kind, and my spirit open to Your leading.

May I be a vessel of Your compassion to those who feel forgotten, a light to those in darkness, and a friend to the lonely.

Bless those who are weary, those who are searching, and those who are hurting.

Wrap them in Your comfort and remind them they are never alone.

Prepare our hearts for the weekend ahead— may it be a time of rest, renewal, and deeper connection with You.

In Jesus' name, **Amen.**

Morning Prayer

Today is August 24, 2025

Lord, as a new day begins, I come before You with an open heart.

You know my life—what worries me, how I feel, what I think, what I long for, what I lack, and what I desire.

In moments of darkness, You are my light.

In storms, You are my peace.

In sadness, You are my strength.

In loneliness, You are my companion.

I hold onto Your promise, for Your Word says:

"Fear thou not; for I am with thee: be not dismayed; for I am thy God: I will strengthen thee; yea, I will help thee; yea, I will uphold thee with the right hand of my righteousness." — Isaiah 41:10 (KJV)

I surrender this day into Your loving hands, knowing You are always with me.

If God is good to you, praise Him.

Amen.

Sunday Prayer

(Written by Fr. Ronald Rey P. Espartinez, SVD)

Almighty Father, thank You for this new day.

Thank You for always standing by my side and reassuring me that Your light will always prevail over darkness.

This Sunday, I pray for a solid faith, trust, and reliance on Your mercy and goodness in my life.

May my heart be filled with the light of faith, so that I will always see and feel Your unfading love toward me despite my limitations, wounds, and pains.

Bless my heart with hope, that I may be filled at all times with a positive mindset, a patient attitude, and a persevering spirit.

By Your grace, help me to become an effective instrument of Your light and compassion to my family and to those in need.

In Jesus' name, **Amen.**

Miracle Prayer

Lord Jesus Christ, I come before You today in need of a miracle.

Touch my life with Your healing hand, for I believe it is Your will for me to be well in mind, body, soul, and spirit.

Cover me with Your precious blood and fill me with Your Holy Spirit.

I ask this in Your holy name.

Amen.

Morning Prayer

August 30, 2025

Heavenly Father, I come before You today asking for forgiveness of my sins.

Lord, thank You for giving me another day to live.

My only request this morning is that You bless my family and friends.

Strengthen their faith.

Let them live with contentment and rejoice in gladness.

Protect them spiritually, physically, mentally, and emotionally.

This I pray in Jesus' name, **Amen.**

Prayer for Tonight

God our Father in heaven, thank You for giving us the gift of prayer.

It is our lifeline to You.

In the moments when we have no one to listen to us, we speak to You in prayer.

Prayer is our refuge and calm, our comfort and forgiveness.

Your power flows through us in prayer.

Prayer is our best refuge and consolation.

We are deeply grateful.

In Jesus' name we pray, **Amen.**

Morning Prayer

Almighty, ever-loving Father, blessed be Your holy name.

We praise and thank You for giving us the golden opportunity to be alive in the land of the living.

In Your boundless goodness and generosity, we humbly ask You to come and dwell within us.

May Your presence adorn us with grace for a life of abundance— in love, gentleness, confidence, strength, honesty, peace, fruitfulness, holiness, and happiness.

Bless our families and friends today.

We ask this through Jesus Christ our Lord.

Amen.

Tonight's Prayer

August 29, 2025

Heavenly Father, as I close this day, I want to thank You for everything You have done in my life, especially for all the blessings and protection You allowed us to experience today.

As we rest tonight, we ask for Your presence to be with us and to keep us safe from harm.

Restore our strength for tomorrow.

We commit everything to You, Lord.

Have Your way in us.

In Jesus' name, **Amen.**

Morning Prayer in Tagalog (Translated)

August 30, 2025 – "PANALANGIN SA UMAGA"

Heavenly Father, we cannot foresee what will happen tomorrow, but we know that everything in this world is under Your control.

Give us faith, so that we will not be afraid in the face of disaster, and so that we may continue to trust in You in the midst of confusion.

Lord, we entrust every day of August into Your hands.

Guide our steps and give us peace and protection.

Whatever happens, we trust in You.

Lord, for the person reading this, please help all their problems to be resolved.

Amen.

Morning Prayer

August 30, 2025 – Saturday

Heavenly Father, as the first light of this Saturday morning shines through, I am overwhelmed with gratitude.

Another day, another opportunity to experience Your grace, mercy, and love.

As I rise, the memory of Your faithfulness throughout the week fills my heart with songs of joy and thanksgiving.

I marvel at the many ways You have shown Your love for me— from the great blessings to the smallest gestures of kindness.

May this Saturday not be just an ordinary day, but a divinely woven series of moments where Your blessings flow abundantly, touching not only me but everyone I encounter.

Amen.

Morning Prayer in Tagalog (Translated)

August 31, 2025

Lord, thank You for the strength You give me each day and for the peace You give my mind.

Lord, may You guide me at all times.

Help me to live each day with joy and love in my heart.

Lord, I ask forgiveness for all my mistakes and shortcomings before You.

I surrender my life to You, and the lives of those I love.

May You reign in our hearts and lead every step of our journey here on earth.

Lord, for the person reading this, please help all their problems to be solved.

Amen.

Morning Prayer in Tagalog (Translated)

August 31, 2025 – Trusting the Future

Heavenly Father, we cannot predict what will happen tomorrow, but we know that everything in this world is under Your control.

Give us faith so that we will not be afraid in the face of calamity and will continue to trust in You amid chaos.

Lord, we entrust every day of August into Your hands.

Guide our steps and give us peace and protection.

Whatever happens, we trust in You.

Lord, for the person reading this, may all their problems be resolved.

Amen.

Sunday Morning Prayer

(Fr. Eva Chibuzo Asadu)

Almighty, ever-living God, we are truly grateful for sustaining us in Your grace throughout the month of August.

Thank You, Lord, for all Your blessings, favors, mercies, tenderness, protection, provision, healing, deliverance, and comfort.

Thank You for supporting us, for feeding us, for nourishing us with good health, happiness, peace, and joy;

for guiding us, rescuing us, and enlightening and empowering us in Your love and grace.

Thank You for the roof over our heads, for our families and friends, for the rain and the sun, for clothing us, and for every victory over struggle and crisis.

As August ends today, Lord, put an end to our misery, sickness, fear, poverty, and pain, through Jesus Christ our Lord.

Amen.

Morning Prayer in Tagalog (Translated)

August 31, 2025 – New Opportunity

This morning, Lord, we thank You for the new opportunity You have given.

Thank You for waking us with new hope and strength.

Bless us throughout this day.

We will continue to trust in You and believe in Your goodness.

Send us wisdom and guidance so that we may stand firm in every trial.

Guide us, Lord, in every step, and show us the path toward the victory we have long prayed for.

May we be a light to others and bring joy and inspiration to those around us.

We dedicate all our decisions and actions in Your name.

We continue to trust and hope for the success we have long awaited.

Amen.

Morning Prayer (Tagalog, Refrain – Translated)

Lord, thank You for the strength You give each day and for the peace in my mind.

Guide me at all times.

Help me live each day with joy and love in my heart.

Lord, forgive all my mistakes and shortcomings before You.

I surrender my life to You, and the lives of those I love.

Reign in our hearts and lead every step of our life here on earth.

Lord, for the person reading this, please help all their problems to be solved.

Amen.

Three Things to Pray Each Morning

For God's Blessing

1st Prayer: Lord, I commit my life, my plans, and my entire day into Your hands.

Take full control of my steps, my words, and my decisions.

Let Your will be done—not mine.

2nd Prayer: I acknowledge that without You I am nothing.

Lead my thoughts, my choices, and my actions according to Your perfect plan— from morning until night.

3rd Prayer: Fill me with Your Holy Spirit.

Protect me from evil.

Renew my strength.

Constantly remind me that You are with me by my side.

You can record this prayer and repeat it each morning.

If you desire a deeper relationship with God, say **Amen** in your heart.

Wednesday Morning Prayer

All-powerful God, You have done all things well.

Thank You for the precious gift of life.

Today we humbly ask You to nourish us with good health, to give us sound mind and body, strength to stand firm, and grace to be resilient.

Grant us wisdom to make good choices and decisions, openness to surrender to Your gracious will, and flexibility to bend our will to Yours.

Give us joy to find peace in You, happiness to appreciate Your love, knowledge and confidence to do what is right, and humility to make unlimited space for Your divine intervention and conversion of heart.

We ask this through Jesus Christ our Lord.

Amen.

When I was lost, Jesus found me.

When I was in sin, Jesus freed me.

When I didn't have the strength to walk, Jesus carried me.

If you love the One who died on the cross to save our souls, say **Amen.**

Morning Prayer

September 4, 2025

Lord, thank You for this new morning.

Thank You for the gift of life and for Your continual love for me and my family.

I pray for protection and guidance, Lord.

Please bless this day ahead.

In Jesus' name, **Amen.**

Today's Prayer – Remembering the Cross

Dear Jesus, thank You for carrying the cross that I could never bear.

By Your sacrifice, I am redeemed.

By Your blood, I am cleansed.

By Your death, I have eternal life.

By Your resurrection, I have hope.

By Your grace, I am forgiven.

By Your mercy, I am accepted.

By Your word, I find the way.

By Your truth, I see the light.

By Your love, I have joy and peace.

Lord, I love You.

I give all honor and glory to You— my Savior, my King, my eternal love.

I promise to share this prayer to glorify You.

If you love Jesus and are not ashamed of Him, say **Amen** in your heart and pass this praise on.

God is so good!

Today Is Thursday

September 4, 2025

God says:

"Do not worry about how tomorrow will be, nor how the future will be.

As long as you rely on Me to live every day, I will surely lead you."

Stop stressing yourself.

God knows what you are facing, and He will help you.

If God has been good to you, say **Amen.**

Friday Prayer

Almighty Father, thank You for creating this earth and for the air that I breathe, which sustains me every day.

Today I pray: help me believe that better days and beautiful things are still to come in my life.

Your love for me has no conditions, and Your generosity has no end for those who believe, hope, and trust in You.

Help me, Father, as I manage the struggles in my life.

Fill my mind and heart with Your divine light and power, so that I may find purpose in my trials and continue to fight the good fight despite everything.

I surrender my all to You, Father— my very existence, my family, my health, and my future security.

Lead me always on Your path.

In Jesus' name, **Amen.**

Tonight's Prayer

September 4, 2025

Dear God, from the bottom of my heart I want to say thank You for everything, especially for taking good care of my loved ones.

Tonight, as we lay our heads to rest, I know that tomorrow is another day and that You will meet all our needs.

In Jesus' name I pray, **Amen.**

Today's Prayer – September 5

We thank You, Father in heaven, that You care for us and that You bind us to Yourself through all Your deeds and all Your help.

We thank You for showing us a way of hope— a way that becomes clearer and firmer under our feet.

On this way, we can defy every evil of this world and time, knowing for certain that everything will come out right and that we will all be brought to the great, eternal goal,

even though we must deny ourselves and go through much suffering.

Your kingdom must come to the glory of Your name, so that all people may live on a higher plane and follow You— the only true help and true life.

Amen.

Prayer for Healing – "Deliver Me from This Sickness"

Dear God,

I am sick and my body is in pain.

I come before You in prayer for healing.

Please stretch forth Your mighty hand over me.

Deliver me from this sickness that is tormenting me.

When fear begins to creep into my heart, fill me with confidence in the power of Your grace.

When I begin to worry about this illness, calm my inner thoughts and give me peace.

In Jesus' name, **Amen.**

God is saying to you today:

THIS IS THE CONFIRMATION

you have been praying for.

You asked for a sign—this is it.

I have heard your prayer.

Something big is coming.

The struggle is over.

I am pouring blessings and miracles over every area of your life.

You are coming out of this.

Food for the Soul – Friday, September 5

Luke 5:33–39

"No man putteth new wine into old bottles; else the new wine will burst the bottles, and be spilled, and the bottles shall perish.

But new wine must be put into new bottles." — Luke 5:37–38 (KJV)

Prayer

Lord Jesus, You make all things new.

Teach me to let go of my old ways and to open my heart to the fresh grace You bring each day.

Fill me with Your Spirit so I can embrace a life renewed in faith, hope, and love.

Amen.

Morning Prayer

September 6, 2025

Dear God, thank You for waking me up to another beautiful day.

I am grateful for Your protection and provision.

Please fill me with peace, strength, and wisdom as I face today's challenges.

May I live in a way that honors You.

In Jesus' name, **Amen.**

Heavenly Father, we praise You for watching over us as we slept through the night.

Thank You for waking us and for the gift of new life today.

Through the special intercession of the Immaculate Heart of the Blessed Virgin Mary, we beg You, O Lord, to purify our hearts from every stain of sin, unbelief, fear, prejudice, vice, bitterness, resentment, malice, grudges, and unforgiveness.

Enrich us with Your grace for holiness and happiness.

We ask this through Jesus Christ our Lord.

Amen.

Sunday Prayer

Almighty Father, thank You for the gift of life.

Please remind me always that You are my beginning and my ultimate end, and that my life will only find its true fulfillment and purpose when I rely on Your unending compassion and love.

Bless me every day with a peaceful mind, a courageous heart, and a soul that faithfully seeks Your light, guidance, and strength.

Help me not to be afraid of facing my imperfections, my past wounds, and my present pains and trials.

Embrace me tightly, Father, when the burdens in my heart and the challenges in my life are too heavy to bear.

Cover me and nourish me with Your saving presence.

In Jesus' name, **Amen.**

Morning Prayer

September 7, 2025

Dear God, thank You for waking me up to another beautiful day.

Thank You for Your protection and provision.

Please fill me with peace, strength, and wisdom as I face today's challenges.

May I live in a way that honors You.

In Jesus' name, **Amen.**

Prayer for Healing – For Friends

Heavenly Father, I come before You in the mighty name of Jesus, lifting up all of my friends who are in need of Your healing touch today.

Lord, You are the Great Physician, and nothing is too hard for You.

Bring healing to broken bodies, strength to weary minds, and peace to troubled hearts.

For those who are in pain, let them feel Your comfort.

For those battling fear or anxiety, surround them with Your perfect peace.

For those who feel weak, restore their strength and renew their hope.

Lord, remind us that by the stripes of Jesus we are healed, and that Your love and mercy never fail.

I declare health, wholeness, and restoration over each life, in Jesus' name.

Amen.

Don't let anyone tell you that you **can't** do something when the Bible clearly says:

"I can do all things through Christ which strengtheneth me." — Philippians 4:13 (KJV)

Amen.

Never Start Your Day Without This Prayer

Dear God, I thank You for giving me a new day.

I pray that You watch over me, my family, and everyone in need of Your grace.

Protect us, guide us, and fill our hearts with Your peace.

Forgive me for my weaknesses and strengthen my faith in You.

Where there is faith, there is love.

Where there is love, there is peace.

Where there is peace, there is God.

And where God is, nothing is missing.

Lord, I place this month in Your hands.

Your plan is always perfect, and Your love never fails.

If you depend on God, say **"I do."**

God Is a Way-Maker

Know this: the God you serve is a way-maker.

He will make a way to get it done, to fix it, to shift it, to turn it— even when there seems to be no way.

Agree with God today that you will serve Him, maintain faith in Him, and wait on Him.

His blessings are always worth the wait and always right on time.

Pray Before You Go to Bed

Dear Heavenly Father, as I prepare to sleep, I come before You asking for peaceful rest.

"I will both lay me down in peace, and sleep: for thou, LORD, only makest me dwell in safety." — Psalm 4:8 (KJV)

Lord, I surrender today's burdens into Your hands, laying down all my worries, fears, and anxieties.

Please watch over me as I rest and cover me with Your peace.

May my body and soul find true rest under Your protection, for I know You are always watching over me and safeguarding my future.

I pray this in Jesus' name.

If God is good to you, praise Him.

Amen.

God Wants You to Read This Verse

Exodus 14:14 (KJV) "The LORD shall fight for you, and ye shall hold your peace."

Everything is going to be alright.

God knows you are tired and that you have done your best.

He understands your worries about the future.

Do not be afraid— He is always watching over you and sees your perseverance and refusal to give up.

God is making a way for you right now.

Don't give up.

You are going to make it, no matter what it looks like right now.

Remember: God is working behind the scenes for your good.

He did not bring you this far to leave you.

Be ready— something you prayed for is about to happen.

Have faith, and you will not have to fight in your own strength.

God will move the wrong people out of the way.

He will open the door you could not open and turn the situation around.

Appendix

MY PERSONAL CHRISTMAS TESTIMONY

The Lesson of the Cow

A few years ago, my wife, my daughter, and I took a pilgrim trip to India. My wife and daughter asked me, "Why do the cows walk around on the road and no cars hit them? How come Indian cows are free?"

I explained that it is because Indian cows are considered holy and worthy of worship; it is illegal to hit a cow in India. Seeing how much we are different in our way of life and thought brings me to a point I force myself to share with you regarding when I was a child.

My best friend was a cow. One of the cows was special; he was a gray color. I called him **"Ai Tow,"** meaning "Gray Cow." I was a cowboy, a herdsman. I took care of over 50 cows daily. I fed them, bathed them, and put them down for a nap.

Sometimes I was deadly tired and fell asleep on the ground because I was only a small boy, four or five years of age. But I had to work to do my chores for my family, and I enjoyed it. Anyway, whenever I fell asleep in the field, Ai Tow gave up his time to eat. He would stand across my body to protect me from harm, ensuring no other cows ran over or stepped on me.

Ai Tow understood me and loved me, perhaps more than some so-called friends who do not comprehend who I am. And yet, though Ai Tow is dead, he remains in my heart. I will never forget his deeds and his love for me.

This is why I never agree with or support any human eating animal meat or using animals to entertain our stupid desires in cruel ways. What about allowing animals to play with us instead of treating them with cruelty? We think they are wild and crazy and kill them. This is why we see elephants killing trainers or sharks killing men—because of the bad karma we did to them. Can we see it and realize it in a simple way?

Again, God makes animals as part of His creation to live with us, to be in "cow-manship" and enjoy one another, not the other way around.

A Prayer of Thanksgiving

Recorded July 4, 2010, at 6:00 AM

Thanks for letting me grow in You. Thanks for giving me strength. Thanks for giving my brain the ability to think of Your Holy Word.

Thanks for Your Spirit, Your Soul, and Your Heart that You provide for me, and that I share with all of Your creation in both human form and nature. Thanks for giving insightful knowledge to realize I am part of Your creation and part of You for a long life and forevermore.

My thanks are endless words to describe what You have provided me. You are not only Father to me but the Provider of everything indeed. And wherever I am, You are there. Thanks for being with me in the timeless Fatherly **ACT** to me and all. This is my word given to me today, that I must record what You have given to me for my life daily.

Thanks for creating Your son and daughter for all nations. I know why today is a special and wonderful day for You to make me realize You. Because it is the Fourth of July, and it is called "free." One part of the nations on earth is America, free from other evil nature controllers.

So now I am a so-called American citizen, part of the modern world. So I must honor the nation where I am. A Nation that Honors God. Because government is instituted by You, God, as Your minister for good. It functions best when leaders honor and obey **HIM**.

Looking back throughout Israel's history, which is our ancient and ancestor human history, God commended those kings for their beliefs and behavior. Since this principle is still applicable today, righteous leaders have a tremendous potential to affect their nations for good. The Lord will guide and support those who fear **HIM** and seek **HIS** wisdom and direction for their decisions.

Love you, God, forever and evermore.

The Bridge of Faith

I do know God. I had been with Him way before I realized it. While I was a Buddhist practicing Dhamma, I knew Jesus. Jesus is the Son of God; God is His Father.

God is everywhere, even in Dhamma. God is in Buddha. God was showing me His quality in the *Brahmaviharas*: **Metta** (loving-kindness), **Karuna** (compassion), **Mudita** (sympathetic joy), and **Upekkha** (equanimity). That is Buddha, who has God inside him, having taught me.

It is such ignorance for one to keep asking the question, "Does God exist?" Yes, God does exist in His form and quality: Love, kindness, sympathy, neutrality, and all forms of humanitarianism. God is there for everyone, including you and me.

God is watching me when I am down. God leaves me alone when I am up. God is seeing me in His eyes when I am in pain. He wipes my tears when I cry. God is profoundly in my heart to comfort me when I am sad. God keeps His eyes on me when I smile. God shares with me when I enjoy myself. God leaves me alone when I am playful and delightful. God leaves me alone when I am performing His good deed and the venture of a Godly act. He is behind me when He knows I will fail to do a Godly act; He is watching me with His own eyes.

Oh God, thanks forever and evermore that You do everything for me in my entire life.

A Litany of Creation

Thanks for letting me learn how to thank You more:

> **Thanks, God, when I eat fruit**, that You created the tree for me.

> **Thanks for the air** You give me to breathe.

> **Thanks for the wind** that blows around my body to feel.

> **Thanks for the white and blue sky**, created in many forms that You designed for me to see, watch, and enjoy.

Thanks for water You give me to drink when I am thirsty, and to clean and wash myself, and clean my clothes and other needed items.

Thanks for the flowers that You have blossom for me to see and smile.

Thanks for the art of different architectural forms You have created for me.

Thanks for the mountain views around the earth that You created for me to hike, to sight around my body, and make my eyes open and enjoy.

Thanks for the Ocean waves, that You proposed the song for them to sing in many songs for me.

Thanks for the beautiful white sand that You provided for me to walk and play on.

Thanks for the fishes that You let swim and play for me to see and enjoy.

Thanks for all the unmeasurable nature You have created just for me and Your sons and daughters.

Thanks for Your loveliness and Your hardest work for Your creation, including myself.

Thanks for all the varieties and species of animals, from the elephant to the small tiny ants, that You created to be with us and for our companionship.

And yet, some of us are misleading and misusing the animals, such as eating them as food or training them as entertainment with so many forms of cruelty. I hate that.

All animals are not for food. For any to be sacrificed as some craziest religious believers do is nothing but morally wrong. But man has wrongly believed and been a wrongdoer for many thousands of years. No one tried to be aware that it is wrong and we must not use animals to be sacrificed in any form of barbarism or belief.

Do not forget, God makes animals to live, not for food to eat. This is why I am a vegetarian, as Hindu teaches me. In Hinduism, animals are holy and worship-able, such as cows. Yes, maybe it is startling for a Westerner when they know that Hindus believe that the cow is holy and worthy of worship. But let us put past ideals in the back of your mind. For thousands of years, there were no tractors. Only cows helped us to do the farm work to grow the rice or hay. For us to eat and survive, without cows, there was no other way to do the farm work.

Cows represent the agency of the Hindu God because they provide the food from the farm for us to live.